RD
HOME
HANDBOOKS

FLOWER
ARRANGING

FLOWER ARRANGING

Contributing editor
Malcolm Hillier

The Reader's Digest Association, Inc.
Pleasantville, New York

This is an RD Home Handbook
specially created for The Reader's Digest Association, Inc.,
by Dorling Kindersley Limited.

First American edition, 1990
Copyright © 1990 by Dorling Kindersley Limited, London
Text copyright © 1990 by Malcolm Hillier and
Dorling Kindersley Limited, London

Published in the United States
by The Reader's Digest Association, Inc.,
Pleasantville, N.Y.
Published in Great Britain
by Dorling Kindersley Limited, London
Printed in Singapore

Designed and edited by Swallow Books,
260 Pentonville Road, London N1 9JY

Library of Congress Cataloging in Publication Data

Flower arranging/contributing editor, Malcolm Hillier.—1st American ed.
        p. cm.—(RD home handbooks)
    ISBN 0-89577-357-0
    1. Flower arrangement—Handbooks, manuals, etc. I. Hillier,
Malcolm. II. Series.
SB449.F557   1990
745.92—dc20
                                                    90-8243
                                                    CIP

CONTENTS

Introduction 6

INTRODUCTION

Flowers play an important part in our lives. Since the beginning of time they have been used to celebrate. Flowers are appropriate to so many occasions, so many different feelings and experiences. A simple bunch given to a friend or someone you love is magical. A decoration in the home for a special event makes an immensely personal statement. In times of happiness flowers can blaze with glory; in serenity, they can be tranquil, and in times of sadness they can bring solace. Their beauty can brighten the most ordinary of days. This book shows you how to introduce some of this beauty into your everyday life. It presents hundreds of inspirational ideas for fresh and dried flower arrangements to suit every occasion and every style of home. It also gives detailed advice on how to choose your flowers and foliage from the vast array of available plant material, and how to use them to create an arrangement for any occasion, simple or grand, formal or informal, summer or winter, and using fresh or dried flowers.

Flowers in the ancient world

The ancient Chinese attributed special meanings to the various plants that grew wild in the countryside and to those they cultivated. They used flowers in religious rituals and originally each arrangement contained only one type of flower. In the spring the peony and peach blossom were most popular; the lotus epitomized summer, and the chrysanthemum, autumn. Plum blossom, white narcissus and pine branches were frequently used in winter.

In celebration of summer
An informal mixture of artemisia, Japanese anemones, delphiniums, sweet peas, spindle, blackberries, pearly everlasting, phlox, roses, montbretia, yarrow, euphorbia, veronica and globe amaranth.

The early Egyptians designed special vases for their flowers and often decorated the vases with floral motifs. The Greeks and Romans always incorporated flowers into their celebrations. They used leaves and flowers in their religious ceremonies, making headdresses, wreaths and garlands for bridal couples, and for heroes and athletes victorious in wars or games. Sometimes, for an assembly, they would strew a whole floor with scented rose petals.

The seventeenth and eighteenth centuries

In the West, the art of arranging flowers was first documented in the seventeenth century, when the Dutch, in particular, painted wonderful informal arrangements of flowers, foliage, fruit and vegetables. Such effects can be recreated today, using great mixtures of brilliantly colorful and scented flowers, combined with beautiful fruits, such as pineapples, pomegranates, mulberries and crab apples, and garden vegetables with interesting shapes, like curly kale, cabbage, beans or peppers.

In the eighteenth century, many potteries produced vases for flowers as well as china for the table. Wedgwood and Sèvres are the best known makers of ceramic flower containers during this period. Arrangements were used to decorate the houses of wealthy families and the aristocracy on a regular basis. Vases of flowers sat on the newly introduced mantelpiece, and in summer a vase of flowers was put in the fireplace, standing on the hearth. Arrangements were also placed on tables, which were brought into the body of the room.

In Britain, the most popular flowers in summer were roses, carnations, irises, peonies, delphiniums, monkshood and hollyhocks. Although

Historical pastiche
An arrangement in seventeenth-century Flemish style, using flowers from different seasons, including lilies, amaryllis, irises, eucomis, hollyhocks, hydrangea, vines, delphiniums, carnations, tulips, tobacco plant, sweet peas, chicory, roses, nerines, poppies, peaches and pomegranate.

the chrysanthemum was introduced from China to the West at this time, it was not until a century later that it became a popular flower, and was used to decorate the house in all manner of flower arrangements.

The nineteenth century
The Victorians retained informality in their arrangements, resulting in some very beautiful, romantic creations in the manner of those painted by Fantin Latour. They used tremendous mixtures of flowers: it was during the nineteenth century that the majority of plant introductions took place and the Victorians were great hybridizers.

They brought to England and the United States many plants from China, Africa and South America. Some of them – like rhododendrons, azaleas, tree peonies, roses and gladioli – have become favorite garden plants. Others – like begonias, calceolarias and fuchsias – were grown under glass and bedded out for the summer months. Plants like carnations and primulas were developed in their thousands to produce very fancy striped and blotched varieties.

Contrasting colors
This cool mixture of blue cornflowers, straw-yellow helichrysum heads and feathery, silvery acacia foliage harmonizes beautifully with the early Delft flower-patterned bowl.

Roses were crossed to produce fabulous blooms with a great number of petals, and most of them were wonderfully scented as well.

But fond as Victorian ladies were of tremendous mixtures of flowers, just as frequently they placed a single type of flower in a vase, either alone or with a few stems of interesting foliage, such as ferns, grasses or bulrushes. It was at this time that striking color contrasts were employed for the first time, and many of these schemes are still in use today.

In the second half of the nineteenth century many books were published on the subject of flower arranging. They contained illustrations of elaborate, wild decorations for dinner parties and special seasonal occasions, including wonderful garlands and swags, and many-tiered epergnes, or ornamental centerpieces, for sideboards or dinner tables. Even Mrs Beeton's *Household Management* includes mention of flower arrangement.

Interest in flower arranging was also developing apace in the United States, where brighter colors and new flower shapes were becoming available, such as dahlias and nasturtiums, azaleas and camellias. At a time when there were few leisure occupations open for women outside the home, women's magazines contained plenty of advice on caring for and displaying cut flowers. It soon became the norm to have arrangements placed in every room.

At the end of the century arrangements became subjects for the Impressionist painters, from Van Gogh with his "Sunflowers" and Bonnard, with a bombardment of rich color, to Manet and Monet. They portrayed flowers in a quite different way, suggesting the scent, color and mood of arrangements rather than painting realistic representations.

Following the seasons
The Flemish and Italian artists of the seventeenth century used artistic licence to fill their vases with a myriad of flowers from every season, but today we can

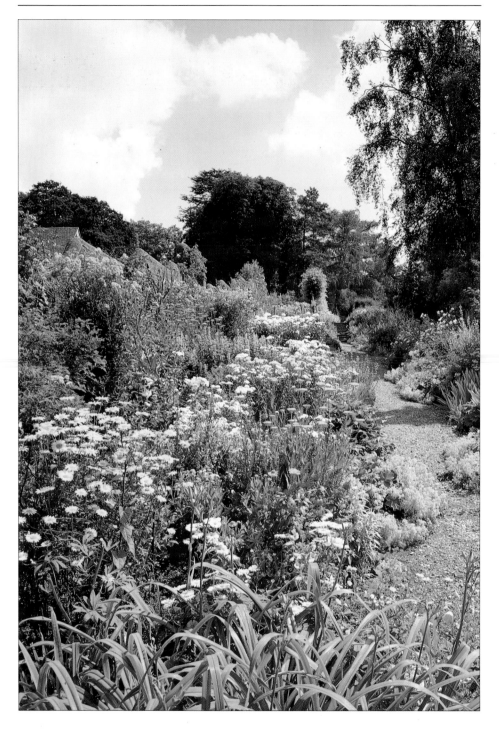

do nearly as well in reality, as more and more flowers become available all year.

Florists now carry not only seasonal flowers but many beautiful and exotic blooms from around the world. Keeping your arrangements seasonal, however, is the way to achieve the most natural-looking results. Early summer is the very best time of year for flowers. Colors are both at their richest and most subtle: reds and blues, peaches, apricots and creams, deep and pale yellows are all offset by the brilliant greens of fresh foliage. Summer is also the time of silver, lilac and pink.

The colors of bonfires and the setting sun are the colors of autumn flowers. In early and midwinter flowers are very scarce. But popping up in the gloom are winter jasmine, the Christmas rose, winter cherry, some of the viburnums and mahonia. Suddenly the grayness begins to lift and soon yellows and white abound, and to echo the spring skies there are touches of clear blue in hyacinth, scilla and iris.

The history of dried flowers

While there is a precious quality about the impermanence of fresh flowers, it is exciting to know that the pleasure they bring can be prolonged. Nearly every plant can be dried or preserved.

When certain flowers and leaves are dried they retain their perfume and these have been used for centuries, both to adorn and perfume rooms. In the seventeenth century nosegays of aromatic plants, often dried, were carried to ward off plague.

In the nineteenth century the imagination of the Victorians was captured by their great plant hunters. Enthusiasts at home made wonderful collections of pressed flowers and leaves and arrangements of dried flowers, grasses and rushes. Then interest in dried flowers gradually waned until by the early 1970s the selection available in shops was limited to just a few grasses, statice and strawflowers, often dyed in unnatural colors.

Border garden
(opposite)
With a large garden you can afford the luxury of wide mixed borders. At the beginning of summer, these borders will yield plentiful yellow and white achillea, delphiniums, and alchemilla.

The revival of interest

About fifteen years ago leading flower arrangers began experimenting with the air drying of blooms and leaves. They found that they could preserve a much greater range of natural colors in the more usual drying flowers than was available ready dried, and they went on to establish a regular supply of roses, delphiniums, larkspur, astilbe, gypsophila and mimosa along with a host of other flowers, grasses, seedheads and leaves.

The list of flowers expanded year after year, and with it an interest was awakened that has now made dried flowers a growth industry. Commercial nurseries all over the world are growing flowers solely for drying, and it is now possible to buy ready-dried flowers native to many distant countries.

Drying techniques

Although air drying is the simplest and most effective method, there are several other ways that plant material can be preserved. Chemical dessicants and sand can be used to draw the moisture from plant material to provide very beautiful, but brittle flowers that keep much of their color and texture. Glycerine can replace the moisture content of many leaves and some flowers, retaining suppleness but often altering colors. Pressing plant material between sheets of absorbent paper is a method of drying that keeps colors true but flattens the material, making it more suitable for mounting under glass. All these techniques are explained in detail in the book.

The flower arranger's garden

If you are fortunate enough to have a garden, it is relatively easy to grow plants that you can harvest and arrange after drying them yourself or while still fresh. Undertaking the whole process of growing, preserving and arranging is a rewarding experience. It is as exciting to dry a few mixed bunches as it is to fill a whole ceiling space with material you have

Overhead view
(above)
This wicker basket is crammed full of field grasses interlaced with yellow helichrysum, anaphalis, helipterum, achillea and silene.

grown. Even in a small garden of 20×30 feet, you can grow enough material to make three or four large dried-flower arrangements. without greatly affecting the look of the garden.

Flowers for drying have to be picked just before they reach perfection. This is an important point when planning your garden. A border should be planted so that it will not look bare when flowers and foliage are harvested for drying. The currently popular mixed border, which contains herbaceous perennials, shrubs, climbers, roses and annuals, is the ideal site for a good selection of plants for drying. However, many rushes and ferns, which provide the fronds, stems and seedheads that are essential to many dried-flower arrangements, tend to prefer very damp soil and are therefore best grown in a separate area of the garden.

The secrets of arranging flowers

The exciting processes of growing and drying flowers, or simply buying bunches of fresh or dried flowers, are merely preliminaries to the creative art of arranging them.

This book will help to demonstrate the techniques that lead to making an arrangement. However, it has to be said that there are no rules for arranging flowers, no lists of fresh or dried flowers that look nice together, no definitive combinations of colors that work better than others. The best advice must be to look to nature for your lead when creating with flowers.

This book shows you the wide range of plant material that can be grown and dried and presents some of the ways this material can be arranged, frequently taking inspiration from the way that plants grow and the shapes they make in the landscape. Some of the arrangements are simple, whereas those for special occasions are more complex. Everyone needs a little inspiration to develop creativity: this book will provide you with just that.

Accent on scent
Of all the freesias, the colored single flowers have the very best clear, sweet perfume.

FRESH
FLOWERS

———

CHAPTER ONE

GUIDE TO FRESH FLOWERS AND FOLIAGE

During the course of the year we are provided with an enormous wealth of plant material. At the end of winter, there is that magic moment when the first crocuses and daffodils appear. Suddenly the fields and gardens come alive with flowers and foliage, the color yellow predominating. In summer the color range changes, with plenty of pink, red and blue flowers and occasional patches of yellow.

Autumn provides more mellow colors: rusts, reds, ambers, golds and oranges dominate the borders, although there are still some pale pinks, creams and white around. In winter there are fewer flowers and we have to rely more on the dark greens of evergreen foliage and the reds of winter berries.

Summer fragrance

The early summer sun warms this basket filled with the loveliest of fresh flowers – delphiniums, peonies, spurge, sweet peas, spiraea, whitebeam, Queen Anne's lace and corn marigolds. The heady fragrance of the peonies and sweet peas heightens the sensual pleasure.

Spring flowers

Lamium
Lamium album

Rosemary
Rosmarinus officinalis

Forsythia
Forsythia × intermedia

Sweet violet
Viola odorata

Orchid
Cymbidium hybrid

Borage
Borago officinalis

Forget-me-not
Myosotis alpestris

Spiraea
Spiraea thunbergii

Kerria
Kerria japonica 'Pleniflora'

European cranberry bush
*Viburnum
opulus 'Roseum'*

Primrose
Primula vulgaris

Primula
Primula denticulata

Daffodil
Narcissus
'Professor
Einstein'

Daffodil
Narcissus
'Sir Winston
Churchill'

Periwinkle
*Vinca
major*

Daffodil
Narcissus
'Passionale'

Daffodil
Narcissus
'Kingscourt'

Daffodil
Narcissus
'Tahiti'

Hyacinth
*Hyacinthus
orientalis*

Daffodil
Narcissus 'Cheerfulness'

Daffodil
Narcissus
'Silver Chimes'

**Grape
hyacinth**
*Muscari
armeniacum*

**Spring
snowflake**
*Leucojum
vernum*

Primrose
Primula
Polyanthus

Cowslip
Primula veris

Comfrey
Symphytum orientale

Skimmia
Skimmia japonica

Decorative crab apple
Malus floribunda

**Decorative
crab apple**
Malus × lemoinei

Pear
Pyrus communis

Primrose
Primula Auricula

Single tulip
Tulipa 'Golden Mirjoran'

Double tulip
Tulipa 'Angelique'

Bethlehem sage
*Pulmonaria
saccharata*

Azalea
Rhododendron cv.

**Decorative
cherry**
Prunus sargentii

Currant
Ribes sanguineum

Anemone
Anemone coronaria
'The Bride'

Flowering quince
Chaenomeles speciosa

Wallflower
Cheiranthus cheiri

Lilac
Syringa vulgaris 'Mme
Florent Stepman'

Camellia
*Camellia
japonica*

Pansy
Viola × wittrockiana

Parrot tulip
Tulipa 'Estella
Rijnveld'

Viburnum
Viburnum carlesii 'Aurora'

Lenten rose
*Helleborus
orientalis*

Star magnolia
Magnolia kobus

Pasqueflower
Anemone pulsatilla

Broom
Cytisus albus

Stinking hellebore
Helleborus foetidus

Italian arum
Arum italicum pictum

Rhubarb
Rheum rhaponticum

Alexanders
Smyrnium olusatrum

Spiraea
Spiraea japonica
'Goldflame'

Common linden
Tilia × europea

Sycamore
Acer pseudoplatanus

Larch
Larix decidua

Spindle
Euonymus japonicus aureus

Honeysuckle
Lonicera periclymenum 'Belgica'

Fig
Ficus carica

Hornbeam
Carpinus betulus

Horse chestnut
Aesculus hippocastanum

Pussy willow
Salix caprea

Mrs Robb's bonnet
Euphorbia amygdaloides robbiae

Lilac
Syringa vulgaris

Summer flowers

Ceanothus
Ceanothus impressus

Columbine
Aquilegia

Candytuft
Iberis

Chives
*Allium
schoenoprasum*

Ranunculus
*Ranunculus
asiaticus*

Laburnum
*Laburnum
× watereri* 'Vossii'

**Bleeding
heart**
*Dicentra
spectabilis*

Clematis
Clematis 'Nellie
Moser'

Snakeweed
Polygonum bistorta

Thrift
Armeria plantaginea

Wood spurge
*Euphorbia
amygdaloides*

Alkanet
Pentaglottis sempervirens

Whitebeam
Sorbus aria
'Lutescens'

Broom
Cytisus × praecox

Jacob's ladder
Polemonium foliosissimum

Queen Anne's lace
Daucus carota

Iris
Iris cv.

Lily-of-the-valley
Convallaria majalis

Spanish bluebell
Scilla hispanica

Allium
Allium albopilosum

Sneezewort
Achillea ptarmica

Stock
Matthiola incana

Fernleaf yarrow
Achillea 'Salmon
Beauty' and
A. 'Moonshine'

Delphinium
Delphinium
Pacific hybrid

Protea
Protea 'Blushing
Bride'

Pinks
Dianthus plumarius
hybrids

Catmint
*Nepeta
grandiflora*

Valerian
Centranthus ruber

Bellflower
Campanula trachelium
'Alba Plena'

Lupine
Lupinus Russell
strain

Lily
Lilium
regale

Rose
Rosa 'Golden
Wings'

Cherry
Prunus avium
'Early Rivers'

Protea
Protea
obtusifolia

Cornflower
Centaurea
cyanus

Asparagus
Asparagus
officinalis

Sweet William
Dianthus barbatus

Snapdragon
Antirrhinum majus

Sweet pea
Lathyrus odoratus

Pink rose
Rosa cv.

Yellow rose
Rosa
'Courvoisier'

Lilac rose
Rosa 'Variegata
di Bologna'

Masterwort
Astrantia major

**Yellow horned-
poppy**
Glaucium flavum

Astilbe
Astilbe
× *arendsii*

Shasta daisy
*Leucanthemum
maximum*

Foxglove
Digitalis purpurea

Allium
Allium aflatunense

Rose
Rosa 'Charles
de Mills'

Mock orange
Philadelphus
'Burfordensis'

White peony
Paeonia lactiflora 'Festiva Maxima'

**Pink
peony**
*Paeonia
lactiflora* cv.

Brodiaea
Brodiaea laxa

Love-in-a-mist
Nigella damascena

Butterfly bush
Buddleia davidii

**Globe
thistle**
Echinops ritro

Heracleum
*Heracleum
mantegazzianum*

Chincherinchee
Ornithogalum thyrsoides

Veronica
Veronica exaltata

**Tobacco
plant**
*Nicotiana
affinis*
'Lime Green'

Statice
*Limonium
sinuatum*

Hibiscus
Hibiscus syriacus
'Woodbridge'

Sweet sultan
Centaurea moschata

Prairie gentian
Eustoma grandiflorum

Clary
Salvia horminum

Monkshood
Aconitum napellus

Meadow-rue
Thalictrum delavayi

Eryngium
Eryngum × oliverianum

Lily
Lilium 'Destiny'

African lily
Agapanthus
Headbourne hybrid

Nectarine
Prunus persica 'Early Rivers'

Lily
Lilium auratum

Mulberries
Morus nigra

Fernleaf yarrow
Achillea filipendulina

Tickseed
Coreopsis

Gayfeather
Liatris callilepis

Sweet pea
Lathyrus latifolius

Lavender
Lavandula angustifolia

Magnolia
Magnolia grandiflora

Pot marigold
Calendula officinalis

Tansy
Tanacetum vulgare

Coneflower
Echinacea purpurea

Baby's breath
Gypsophila paniculata

Bouvardia
Bouvardia × domestica

Freesia
Freesia × kewensis

Gerbera
Gerbera jamesonii

Strawflower
Helichrysum bracteatum

Penstemon
Penstemon hartwegii

Honeysuckle
Lonicera periclymenum serotina

Phlox
Phlox paniculata

Montbretia
Crocosmia pottsii

Protea
Banksia menziesii

Opium poppy
Papaver somniferum

Godetia
Clarkia grandiflora

Cockscomb
Celosia argentea cristata

Black-eyed Susan
Rudbeckia hirta
'Double Gloriosa'

Peruvian lily
Alstroemeria ligtu
hybrid

Carnation
Dianthus caryophyllus
'Scarlet Elegance'

Larkspur
Delphinium elatum

Currant
Ribes sanguineum

White poplar
Populus alba

Barberry
Berberis thunbergii
'Rose Glow'

Hebe
Hebe armstrongii

Caladium
Caladium × hortulanum

Spindle
Euonymus japonicus

Rose
Rosa glauca

Sword fern
Nephrolepsis exaltata

Artemisia
Artemisia ludoviciana

Cotton lavender
Santolina chamaecyparissus

Wood spurge
Euphorbia amygdaloides

Senecio
Senecio 'Sunshine'

Hosta
Hosta forunei
'Aureomarginata'

Kerria
Kerria japonica

**Bells of
Ireland**
*Moluccella
laevis*

Fig
Ficus carica

Lamb's ears
Stachys byzantina

Rue
Ruta graveolens

Lady's mantle
Alchemilla mollis

Dogwood
Cornus alba
'Elegantissima'

Autumn flowers

Acidanthera
Gladiolus callianthus

Strawberry tree
Arbutus unedo

Sweet corn
Zea mays

Michaelmas daisy
Aster ericoides
'Monte Casino'

Chrysanthemum
Chrysanthemum
'Statesman'

Chrysanthemum
Chrysanthemum
'Evelyn Bush'

Bouvardia
Bouvardia × domestica

St John's-wort
Hypericum calycinum

Milkweed
Gomphocarpus

Statice
Limonium latifolium

Tickseed
Coreopsis

Dryandra
Dryandra sp.

White potato vine
Solanum jasminoides album

Goldenrod
Solidago
'Goldenmosa'

Bear's breeches
Acanthus spinosus

Crab apple
Malus 'Yellow Siberian'

Boneset
Eupatorium sp.

Globe amaranth
Gomphrena globosa

Vervain
Verbena × hybrida

Pink nerine
Nerine bowdenii

Scabious
Scabiosa caucasica

Cup and saucer vine
Cobaea scandens

Lily
Lilium speciosum rubrum

Chinese gentian
Gentiana sino-ornata

Pale-pink fuchsia
Fuchsia cv.

Plume thistle
Cirsium japonicum

Cupid's dart
Catananche caerulea 'Major'

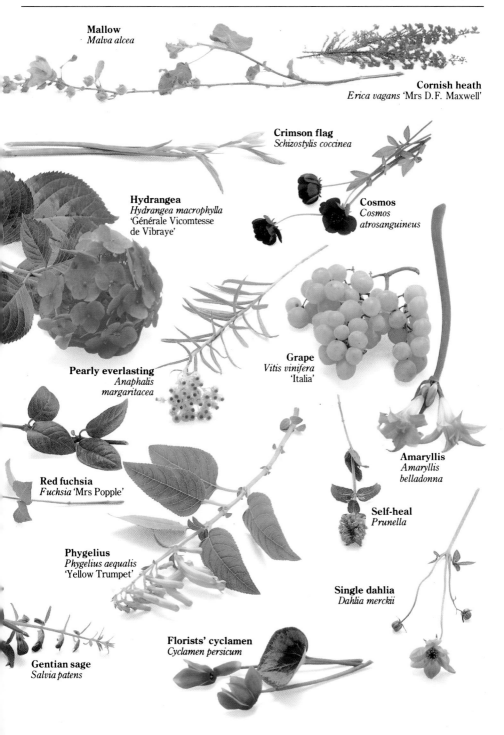

Mallow
Malva alcea

Cornish heath
Erica vagans 'Mrs D.F. Maxwell'

Crimson flag
Schizostylis coccinea

Hydrangea
Hydrangea macrophylla
'Générale Vicomtesse
de Vibraye'

Cosmos
*Cosmos
atrosanguineus*

Grape
Vitis vinifera
'Italia'

Pearly everlasting
*Anaphalis
margaritacea*

Amaryllis
*Amaryllis
belladonna*

Red fuchsia
Fuchsia 'Mrs Popple'

Self-heal
Prunella

Phygelius
Phygelius aequalis
'Yellow Trumpet'

Single dahlia
Dahlia merckii

Florists' cyclamen
Cyclamen persicum

Gentian sage
Salvia patens

Love-lies-bleeding
Amaranthus caudatus

Waratah
Telopea sp.

Chrysanthemum
Chrysanthemum indicum

Dahlia
Dahlia
'Nina Chester'

Ornamental pepper
*Capsicum annuum
acuminatum*
'Friesdorfer'

Chrysanthemum
Chrysanthemum
'Mason's Bronze'

Michaelmas daisy
Aster novae-angliae

Chrysanthemum
*Chrysanthemum
indicum*
'Charming'

Chinese lantern
*Physalis alkekengi
franchetii*

Gladioli
Gladiolus nanus
'Peter Pears'

Chrysanthemum
Chrysanthemum indicum

Sedum
Sedum spectabile

Pitcher plant
Sarracenia sp.

China aster
Callistephus chinensis

Japanese anemone
Anemone × hybrida
'Honorine Jobert'

Dried pomegranate
Punica granatum

Dryandra
Dryandra drummondii

Snowdrop tree
Halesia monticola

European Cranberry
Viburnum opulus

Horse chestnut
Aesculus sp.

Firethorn
Pyracantha coccinea
'Lalandei'

Stranvaesia
Photinia davidiana

Barberry
Berberis thunbergii
atropurpurea

Rose hips
Rosa cv.

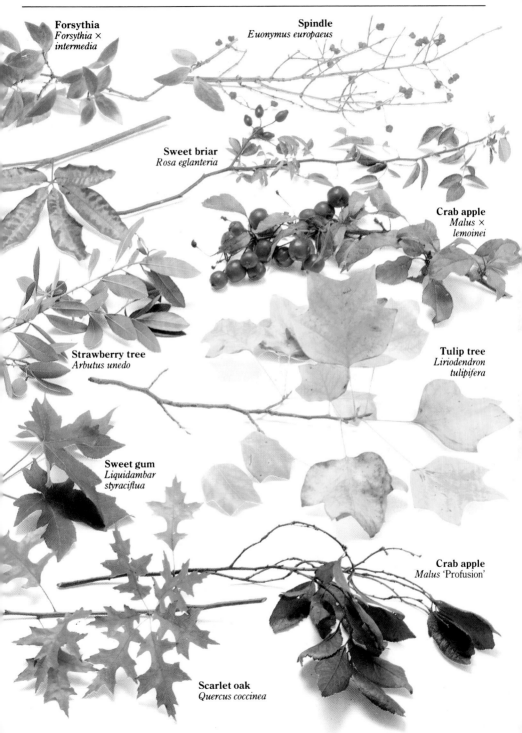

Forsythia
*Forsythia ×
intermedia*

Spindle
Euonymus europaeus

Sweet briar
Rosa eglanteria

Crab apple
*Malus ×
lemoinei*

Strawberry tree
Arbutus unedo

Tulip tree
*Liriodendron
tulipifera*

Sweet gum
*Liquidambar
styraciflua*

Crab apple
Malus 'Profusion'

Scarlet oak
Quercus coccinea

Winter flowers

Daphne
Daphne odora

Silk tassel bush
Garrya elliptica

Heather
Erica × darleyensis
'Darley Dale'

Euphorbia
Euphorbia fulgens

Wintersweet
Chimonanthus praecox

Primula
Primula obconica

Viburnum
Viburnum × bodnantense

Snowdrop
Galanthus nivalis

Winter aconite
Eranthis hyemalis

Witch hazel
Hamamelis mollis

Winter heliotrope
Petasites fragrans

Shrub honeysuckle
Lonicera × purpusii

Poinsettia
Euphorbia pulcherrima

Laurustinus
Viburnum tinus

Mahonia
Mahonia × media
'Charity'

Hellebore
Helleborus argutifolius

Iris
Iris danfordiae

Iris
Iris unguicularis

Winter jasmine
Jasminum nudiflorum

Elaeagnus
Elaeagnus pungens 'Maculata'

Griselinia
Griselinia littoralis

Hemlock
Tsuga canadensis

Yew
Taxus baccata

Cotoneaster
Cotoneaster
'Cornubia'

Camellia
Camellia japonica

Shallon
Gaultheria shallon

Mahonia
Mahonia × *media* 'Charity'

Skimmia
Skimmia japonica

Mrs Robb's bonnet
Euphorbia amygdaloides robbiae

Senecio
Senecio 'Sunshine'

Portugal laurel
Prunus lusitanica

Southern beech
Nothofagus betuloides

Blue spruce
Picea pungens glauca

Holly
Ilex aquifolium

Parchment-bark
Pittosporum tobira
'Variegatum'

Ivy
Hedera helix

Rosemary
Rosmarinus officinalis

Japanese aralia
Fatsia japonica

Lawson's cypress
*Chamaecyparis
lawsoniana* 'Lutea'

CHAPTER TWO

PRINCIPLES OF FRESH FLOWER ARRANGING

There is no need to find the thought of creating an arrangement of fresh flowers intimidating. Although there are no hard and fast rules about what will look attractive, there are some guidelines that you may find useful. Whichever type of arrangement you wish to make, it is simply a matter of choosing a group of flower shapes and foliage that go well together, and whose colors work with the style and the decoration of the room in which the arrangement will be placed. The scale of an arrangement is important too, especially if it is to be seen by a large group of people. Choose a container that will complement both flowers and foliage, and the room, and, lastly, consider the scent of the plant material you plan to use.

These factors are not nearly as restricting as they may at first sound. Flowers are so beautiful that almost any combination of forms and colors is bound to look attractive.

Complementary container

An abundant arrangement in a blue and white faïence cachepot stands before a doorway into the courtyard of Ightham Mote in Kent, England. The delphiniums pick up the blue of the design amidst a sea of white dill, pale-green maidenhair fern, a sprinkling of yellow alstroemeria and the stems of tea tree.

Style

Before starting to create an arrangement of flowers, think about where you want to position it and how it will relate to the designs, colors, forms and textures around it. Consider the space that will surround the arrangement and how that space is used. This will give you an idea of the scale and size it should be.

If it is to stand on a hallway table, then it must be large enough to be noticed, but it must not be so wide that it obstructs people walking through the hall.

If the arrangement is to go on a dining table, then it must look attractive from the points of view of all the diners, and it must not take up too much of the table, making the place settings or serving areas cramped. Most importantly, it must not obstruct the view of the guests. This does not mean that it cannot be tall, but if it is tall it must be narrow, with the flowers held above eye level.

If it is for a bedside table, then leave space for a book and for leaning across to check the time or turn off the alarm clock.

Low arrangement for a coffee table
The contrast between the pink tulips and the blue bowl gives this low arrangement dramatic interest. The stems have been cut short to keep the tulips compact and bushy.

An arrangement for a coffee table should look good from above and every side. It should not take up too much room: you may want to place coffee cups on the table after dinner. A shelf arrangement should not look cramped beneath the shelf above it. Remember that in any situation, the flowers should always have space to declare themselves attractively. An arrangement for a fireplace rarely looks good fitted into the grate of the fire. It is much better to stand it on the hearth in front of the grate. Remember that it will probably be seen from the sides as well as the front.

Matching the decorations

Always take into account the atmosphere of the room. Chrome and modern glass rarely look attractive in a Victorian or chintzy setting, whereas they can look very special against old well-worn wood, such as oak, as well as in a modern room. If the decorations are somber, rich-colored flowers and containers look best. In a pastel room, pale flowers, with touches of bright color, are ideal.

Although an arrangement should relate to the style and decoration of the room in which it is placed, be wary of matching flowers to decorations exactly: there can often be something very calculated about such arrangements.

Echo and offset the colors of your rooms with your flowers, simply by avoiding using colors that seem to you to look unattractive together. Sometimes it will be the color of the wood in your room or the pattern of your curtains, carpet or wallpaper that gives you the idea for a combination of flowers. At other times it will be the mix of flowers outside in the garden. Whatever prompts you to choose certain flowers and shapes, be bold in them.

Flowers and houses

Although flowers are amazingly adaptable, the age and style of the building can substantially influence arrangements.

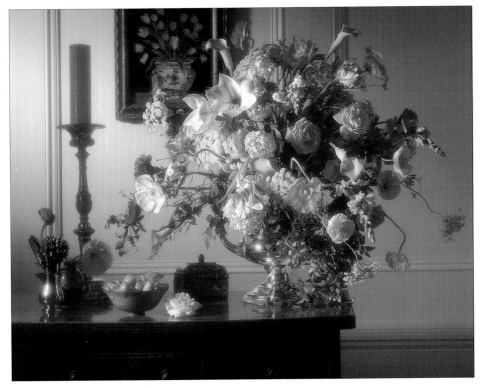

Contemporary houses, especially those with large plate glass windows and minimalist decorations, generally suggest simple and unfussy arrangements, maybe using only one type of flower, and possibly using just one color as well. The containers, too, should be simple in both shape and form to create the best effect.

However, many of the houses now being built have a neo-Classical character and these need more traditional arrangements. That is not to say that these arrangements must be formal, but they should have some of the elegance of the period. Likewise the containers need not be originals, but neither should they be starkly modern.

As well as bearing in mind the period of the house, make sure that the proportions of the arrangement are suitable, so that it relates to the height of the ceiling and the room size. So in a well-proportioned town house, for example, you can afford to create more extravagant flower

Relaxed elegance for a traditional setting
A silver wine cooler makes a gleaming container for this wonderful mix of Iceland poppies, roses, amaryllis, parrot tulips, cranberry bush, carnations, snapdragons, broom, Queen Anne's lace, arum lilies and similax. The studied, informal look of the arrangement is accentuated by the cleverly positioned crooked stems and casual hanging flowers.

arrangements, which in a smaller modern house would look out of place. Simple combinations of flowers look best, no matter what the setting; arrangements should always look natural and never appear to have been tortured into shape. With this in mind it follows that a simple pitcher arrangement can look equally at home in a contemporary or traditional setting, but whereas one type of flower, such as yellow lilies or stems of lilac, would look best in the contemporary room, a mixture of simple country flowers and foliage would be better suited to the traditional setting.

Grand arrangements

Large-scale arrangements are often created for special occasions where a large number of people are expected and the flower arrangements must be both tall and wide in order to be seen. They are often made to display on a pedestal.

A grand arrangement is one that stands at least 3 feet tall. Although it is possible to cut foliage this long, the stems of flowers are frequently shorter. To overcome the problem, short-stemmed material is placed in funnel-like tubes, filled with water. The tubes are either inserted in the foam or wire base in the vase or, for even greater height, attached to lengths of cane, which are then fixed in the foam.

Most large arrangements are fan shaped, although this depends entirely on how many sides of the arrangement will be viewed. If, as is often the case, the arrangement is to be set against a wall, it will need to be flat-backed. If, however, the arrangement is to be placed near the pulpit or the main doors of a church, it may well need to be an all-around arrangement.

For a large space in a large building, where the flowers will be seen from afar, the plant material used in an arrangement should be bold: strong-shaped leaves and vibrant flowers are essential if your creation is to make an impact.

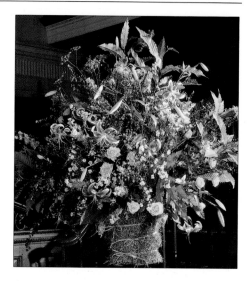

Church pedestal arrangement
This majestic arrangement includes flowers which will stand out in the dark interior. It is composed of sweet chestnut and barberry foliage with fennel, Michaelmas daisies, 'Golden Times' roses, montbretia, larkspur and 'Uchida' lilies.

Making the arrangement (below)
First cover a wastepaper basket with hay (see p. 181), then pack in wet foam. Insert three funnels into the foam. Arrange the long-stemmed foliage in the foam in a fan shape. Add the taller flowers. Finally, pack shorter flowers and foliage in the funnels for height.

Color

From day to day we do not take a great deal of notice of the colors that surround us: the trees and gardens, the walls in the rooms in which we live, or the fruit and vegetables at the produce market. We notice color only occasionally, perhaps when we come to decorate or furnish a room, or when we dress for a special event. We should become more conscious of color, and what better tutor than flowers? They grow in an extraordinary array of hues.

Do not be frightened by color, sticking only to "safe" but boring combinations. Instead, why not experiment with using different colors? Then gradually you will come to know instinctively which colors work best together. At worst, you will create a haphazard medley of flowers or a

Vibrant color contrast
Rich, strongly contrasting colors work together here in a lively flower combination that would look good against almost any background. The striking yellow of the tansy heightens the pinks, reds and lilacs of Peruvian lilies, statice, viburnum and melaleuca.

closely matched understatement, and both of these can look beautiful in the right setting. At best, and most often, you will create an arrangement with an inexplicable but joyful touch of magic, for flowers have a way of making this happen.

Color theory

There are are no hard and fast rules that govern the use of color in arrangements, although the seasonal rules offer some guidance – try using a bright mix of colors in summer, warm mellow hues in autumn, harder lines of browns and dark greens for winter and clear white, yellows and blues in spring.

Alternatively, take your cue from the color spectrum. There are three primary colors in the color spectrum – red, yellow and blue – and different combinations of these make the secondary colors – orange, green and purple. Varying shades and tones of all these colors are created by mixing them with white or black.

Adding drama to an arrangement (left)
The delphiniums bring just the right amount of blue to this large-scale, all-around, floor-standing arrangement in a handsome terracotta pot. The other flowers are white roses, statice and chrysanthemums 'Tokyo' and 'Tuneful'; the foliage is feathery bottlebrush and glossy Mexican orange blossom.

Coordinating flowers and container (above)
This spring arrangement is informally displayed in an old Spanish bowl whose colors mix well with the cream of the heath and narcissi and the blue grape hyacinths and forget-me-nots. The arrangement is strengthened by the pussy willow twigs while splashy pink rhododendrons enhance the cool colors.

The closer together colors are in the spectrum, the more likely they are to mix easily. You cannot go far wrong by mixing red and orange, or orange and yellow, yellow and green, green and blue, and blue and violet. This is all very well but close color combinations can lack drama and there should be at least a little tingle of excitement in every flower arrangement.

Add excitement by choosing colors farther apart in the spectrum. Mixtures of yellow and violet, and orange and blue can look stunning. Such daring combinations should be exploited sometimes.

There are a few colors that look awful together. Some differing blues look un-comfortable when juxtaposed, and dull orange can be difficult to use successfully as

it often seems to remove the clarity of the colors near to it. In truth, though, most flower colors mix with ease and it is more a question of knowing *how much* of each color to include to make the arrangement a pleasing whole and an exciting combination. Of course, the flowers should also relate to and not clash with the color of the decor. So take the main colors of the room as your points of reference.

Matching colors to containers

The relationship between the color of the container and the color of the flowers placed in it is very important. They must work together, for the arrangement is composed of both flowers and container, and each is as important as the other.

Foliage shape and color
Foliage is often even more varied in shape and form than flowers. This arrangement displays a diverse combination of stripes, curves, spikes, clusters and colors in a mix of Bells of Ireland, fan palm, angel wings, gaultheria, oats and milkweed.

Subdued, rustic containers like baskets will carry most combinations of flowers, whereas a brightly colored ceramic vase might overpower many flowers.

Similarly shaped arrangements in the same container will have profoundly different effects because of the use of color. Pastel flowers create a shimmering, misty look, while deep reds and pinks, for example, make a more emphatic statement.

However dramatic the container you choose to use, the most important thing is that the arrangement of flowers and foliage must appear inevitable.

The importance of foliage
Green is the odd man out in the color spectrum as far as plant material is concerned because it is the color of foliage. It always seems to exist happily with any of the other colors. In fact, it strengthens and vitalizes other colors, particularly those that are strong in tone, such as red, bright blue and yellow.

The greens of foliage are tremendously important in arrangements. They bring to life the colors of the flowers with which they are arranged. There are so many different shades to choose from: the golden yellow greens of elaeagnus, euonymus, privet and griselinia; the rich, bright greens of beech, oak, fern fronds, palm leaves, pittosporum, camellia and rhododendron; the silvery green leaves of rosemary, *Senecio* 'Sunshine', lavender, santolina and artemisia; and the dark, heavy greens of yew, box and holly. Leaf shapes vary enormously, from the fine needles of pine to the complicated latticework fronds of fern, and from the large-fingered leaves of fig to the feathery leaves of mountain ash. All contribute to an arrangement. Indeed,

Single-color arrangement
The almost monotonal combination of dusty-orange gladioli and autumnal oak foliage in an austere stoneware jar would best suit a modern interior.

a skilful arrangement featuring only foliage can look truly splendid.

Try to use a lot of green, especially the foliage of the flowers in the arrangement. It is better to limit the flowers than the foliage, as foliage gives a natural growing look to every arrangement. It offsets the forms the color of the flowers that it is mixed with just as it does in the countryside or garden, where green is always the predominant color, even during winter.

Shape

The very simplest kind of flower arrangement is the bunch. There are two sorts of "arranged" bunches: the nosegay in which the flowers are arranged in a circular fashion, to be seen from all sides; and the bouquet, in which the flowers are set out in a fan shape and designed to be seen only from the front.

By arranging nosegays and bouquets in vases you create two of the simplest forms of container arrangement. From a nosegay you can make an all-around arrangement suitable for an occasional table, and from a bouquet you can make a flat-backed arrangement for standing against a wall.

All-around arrangements

Whether circular or oval, low and simple or very tall and complicated, all-around arrangements look equally good from any

An all-around arrangement
This perfectly proportioned basket of flowers is an ideal centerpiece for a country dining table.

1 *Fix a florist's prong to the base of a plastic container with adhesive clay. Place the container in the basket and secure wet foam onto the prong.*

2 *Make the basic all-around curve shape with eucalyptus, turning the arrangement as you work. The stems should appear to spring from the lower center and rise above the handle. Add the carnations informally, keeping the curve.*

3 *Following the line of the curve, add the ice-pink larkspur. Next, add the bright-pink orchids, the delicately arching prairie gentians and the deep red godetias. Stand back to view the whole arrangement and add ingredients to fill out the shape. Fill with water so the flowers last as long as possible.*

angle. They are particularly suitable for freestanding tables such as dining tables or coffee tables, or for any location where the vase is not positioned close to a wall. Many people prefer this type of arrangement – it is lovely to be able to see through to the flowers and foliage at the back.

The best containers for all-around creations are the cylindrical and round-topped ones. Square and wide, elliptic and rectangular containers can also be suitable, and can vary from very low to quite tall vases. Narrow vases are not so well suited to this type of arrangement and are much more effective when used for one-sided, or facing, arrangements. However, most baskets, pitchers and mugs are appropriate, as are most materials.

The correct height of an all-around arrangement depends on its situation. For instance, a low arrangement is best in the center of a dining table, so that it does not block the view of guests across the table. However, for a wide side table or to divide a room, a much taller all-around arrangement will be most attractive.

Facing arrangements

Flower arrangements that are placed against a wall where the back of the arrangement cannot be seen are known as facing, or flat-backed, arrangements. For them to work successfully, it should appear as though they are really all-around arrangements when seen from either the front or the sides. It is never attractive for these flat-backed arrangements to be placed *directly* against the wall, unless it is absolutely necessary because of restricted space, as they can easily lose their three-dimensional feel if they are too narrow. One-sided arrangements probably look at their best when they are placed against a wall or in front of a mirror.

Flat-backed arrangements do, of course, save on the number of flowers needed, as you are only looking at the display from one side. The flowers at the sides of an altar can be displayed in this way, thus saving on material. So, too, can a flower arrangement for a mantelpiece, a hall table, or a floor-standing arrangement for the corner of a room. However, the smaller the arrangement becomes, or the closer to the ground it is to stand, the more unlikely it is that you will be able to use such an arrangement, as the back will be visible.

To arrange a flat-backed flower display, it is easiest to start with foliage first. Place this at the back of the arrangement, in a rough fan shape, level with the back of the vase. Then fill in with more foliage toward the front, before finally adding the flowers that you have decided to use.

Dining-table arrangement
This would make an unusual centerpiece for a large dining table. The base is a large plate covered with wet foam topped with moss. Stems of narcissi, tulips, ranunculus and ivy are then pushed through the moss into the foam.

A facing arrangement
Flat-backed flower arrangements suit positions where the back is not visible. This arrangement is attractively displayed on a shelf at eye level.

1 *Fill the container with wet foam. Then arrange camellia leaves and asparagus fern in a fan shape at the back of the container. Use the remainder of the foliage to fill in at the front.*

2 *Cut the miniature orchid stems into two sections and place with the cream freesias in the wet foam, following the shape of the foliage.*

3 *Add the roses, broom and Peruvian lilies. The stems of Peruvian lilies can be split into five or six pieces, and as these are the most delicate it is best to insert them last.*

Fragrance

Every bit as important as color and form, the perfume of flowers varies from sweet and delicate to strong and spicy. Take every chance to use scented flowers in your arrangements and in any gift of bouquets and nosegays you offer. A room perfumed with flowers is wonderful, and there is nothing nicer than to receive a present of flowers that not only look beautiful but impart their delicious and highly individual scents to a room.

Spring and summer scents

Spring arrangements can be full of scent. There are the delicious hyacinths and many of the varieties of narcissus, especially jonquils and the very popular 'Actea'. But when thinking of scented flowers, roses are the first that come to mind.

Although roses with little or no scent can be used in arrangements for their unusual colors or shapes, try to incorporate at least a few roses with that delicious sweet, fruity "tea" scent in your summer arrangements: that scent is what summer is all about. The earliest flowering roses, such as the simple varieties like 'Canary Bird', tend to have little or no scent. Fortunately, however, the powerfully scented lily-of-the-valley also flowers at this time. As well as looking beautiful in an arrangement, they more than make up for the lack of scent in the roses.

Accent on scent
Two perfumes emanate from this simple arrangement. The sweet scent of the hyacinths carries beautifully in the air, whereas you need to draw close to the violets to smell their delicate perfume.

Perfumes of springtime
*There are a host of spring flowers with delicious scents
that can be used in arrangements to perfume your
rooms. Here (from left to right) are: buttery-scented
grape hyacinths and sweet primroses; spicy hyacinths
and mimosas; violets; aromatic wax flowers and sweet
lily-of-the-valley; and, finally, peppery tulips with
sprays of heady lilac. Other spring flowers with
sweet perfumes include narcissus and pushkinia.*

If you are lucky enough to live in an area
where the climate is mild, you can grow
Rosa banksiae – so profuse in Italy and the
south of France – with its fragrance of rich
violets. Its little creamy-yellow flowers are
a delight to look at and its scent, sheer joy.
Some of the best scents, however, belong
to the old roses: the heady-scented
Damasks and Hybrid Musks, the clear,
sweet-scented Rugosas and, from among
the China roses, those with a rich tea
scent. More and more roses are now being
produced that have both the beautiful looks
of the old-fashioned roses, with their flat,
well-quartered flowers, and delicious
scents. This makes a welcome change after
several decades of roses produced only for
their Hybrid Tea shapes, which often had
little or no scent.

Few people are aware that at this time
of year, irises have a very special perfume.
The scent has a strange quality about it,
often very sweet and violet-like with a
slight rubbery smell on top. It sounds
horrible but it isn't at all. Then there are the
sweet peas. Their flower petals resemble
butterflies and, like butterflies, their
perfume wafts lightly and delicately on the
air, one small bunch easily scenting a room.

With the arrival of high summer come
the pinks, with their clove scents, and the
lilies. Strongest scented of all the lilies are
the auratum lilies, whose scent is very
nearly overpowering: richly spicy, like
concentrated nutmeg and vanilla. The
perfume of nicotiana is similar, although
not quite so heavy. Surprisingly, its flowers
last quite well after picking and are ideal
for arrangements.

Autumn and winter scents
Autumn flowers tend to be better known
for their vibrant colors and abundant
blooms than their fragrance. None the less,
in autumn, the belladonna lily with its pink
or white blooms is in flower, giving out a
sugary, medicinal scent. Also at this time,

the long-lasting *Lilium speciosum rubrum*, with its toffee-scented blooms, adds fragrance to a floral display.

In winter no garden is complete without winter-sweet – *Chimonanthus praecox*. This is a deciduous wall shrub that looks rather ordinary for most of the year, but in midwinter produces a crop of beautiful creamy, waxlike bells with a really strong fragrance, reminiscent of gardenias. Unfortunately, it takes a few years to

flower, but it is well worth a place in the garden, as a few flowering twigs brought inside will perfume a room for several days. Winter heliotrope is another winter-flowerer; it produces stems of delicate pink flowers with a honeylike scent, which are surrounded by unusual, almost circular, leaves.

In late winter, witch hazel – *Hamamelis mollis* – grows strange, spidery, yellow flower petals with the most delicious scent.

Perfumes of summertime
Summer is the sweetest time of year for scent. The most fragrant summer flowers of all are the sweet peas and roses, but peonies, irises and pinks also have lovely perfumes. Why not take the opportunity to give someone a nosegay or bouquet of scented flowers to fill their home with summer fragrance?

Tea roses (below)
This simple bunch has a gloriously fruity scent.

Lilies (right)
Their opulent fragrance is especially strong in the evenings.

Sweet peas (right)
These delicate blooms have a unique sweetness.

Tuberoses and honeysuckle (below)
Combined with lemon-scented geranium leaves, they make a heady perfume.

Lavender and rosemary (right)
The authentic scent of a traditional cottage garden.

Stocks and phlox (left)
Two highly scented flowers for an intensely spicy bouquet.

Freesias (right)
The colored single flowers have the best perfume.

Choosing containers

Every flower arrangement that we create in a container is like a three-dimensional painting set on the wall of a room, and it is the *whole* effect of the flowers and container, and their relationship to the surroundings that is important. Flower arrangements have an advantage over still-life paintings, though: they do not last for ever so there is no chance of becoming bored with them.

The combination of flowers and container is crucial to the success of the arrangement. Sometimes flowers will cry out for a particular container and sometimes a container will immediately suggest a selection of flowers to be arranged in it. So a coffee cup decorated with roses, for example, seems perfect filled with matching old-fashioned roses. Equally, lavender and clary will look especially attractive in a basket made from

Wicker-basket container
The wheat complements the texture of this basket while contrasting strongly with the successful combination of bright anemones and rich hydrangeas.

lavender stems. Sometimes it will be the colors and texture of a container that suggest which flowers to use in the arrangement. Of course, it is not always possible to fill a container with exactly the flowers it demands, but it is good to try.

Arrangements always work best when the container and the flowers seem absolutely meant for each other; where colors and forms complement each other, from the shape and decorations of the vase to the flowers and leaves themselves. Certainly, there are many containers that are unexacting.

Ceramic containers

The range of ceramics you can use is enormous. In general, plain-colored vases or those with abstract or geometric designs, rather than those that are over-decorated with flowers, are the most satisfactory in which to create arrangements. If you have an attractively shaped vase with an ugly pattern or design, remember that you can cover it with some cloth or plant material.

Many combinations of flowers will look good in ceramic vases in shades of white. However, shape is important here. Allow the form of the vase to dictate the shape of the arrangement. A bulbous goldfish bowl of a vase invariably requires a generously curved creation, whereas a tall, straight-sided vase demands tall, straight spires of flowers. This is not to say that it would be impossible to do the reverse, but it is safer to follow this guide.

Using baskets

Basket shapes vary from the traditional, deep, flower-gathering trug to square ones designed for shopping. All can be lined and used for floral arrangements.

Baskets always look attractive filled with flowers, especially the more rustic, twiggy ones, which are made all over the world. All sorts of plant material are used to make these baskets, from the traditional willow

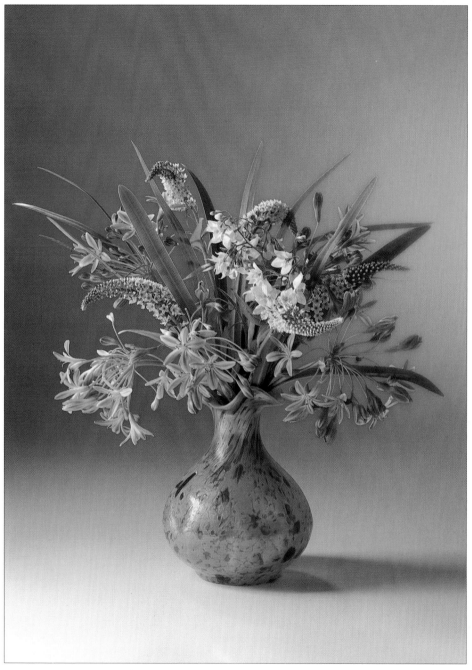

Vase dictates form
The stems of the blue African lily continue the curve of *this art nouveau vase and twisting spires of loosestrife* *and sprigs of solanum echo the theme.*

Glass sugar bowl
The brilliant blue of these gentians needs no enhancement so the simple, understated glass bowl makes an ideal container for this breakfast tray.

Earthenware (right)
These huge, proud sunflowers still seem to spring straight from the soil when viewed in this roughly shaped, semiglazed example of peasant pottery.

Cup and saucer (below)
A fine china Belleek cup and saucer make the perfect container for an exciting arrangement of spurge, sweet pea, lavender, wild pansy, lavender cotton, tricyrtis, lamium and mint. The green of the spurge echoes the shamrock on the white glaze.

to scented thyme and lavender branches, and from olive and bamboo to palm and vines. A basket *is* plant material, and that is why a plant looks so appropriate in one.

Household items

You need not confine your floral arrangements to conventional vases or baskets. Keep a constant look-out for simple household receptacles, such as cups, mugs, pitchers, wastepaper baskets and casseroles, all of which can be used to good effect. Eighteenth- and nineteenth-century pieces of china make lovely containers and can be inexpensive, especially if they are cracked. They can always be lined if they leak and if the vase is beautiful, the cracks add authenticity.

Similarly, it is not always easy to find metal and stone containers, though you may have a wine cooler, attractive cookie jar,

tea cannister or stone mortar tucked away in the kitchen that can be brought into service as a flower container. Copper bowls and brass cachepots also make good containers.

Glass vases

Glass is a wonderful medium for flowers. Clear glass containers, so long as the stems of your flowers are in good condition, can show off your arrangement very effectively. Depending on the shape of the vase, the stems become magnified.

Glass containers range in shape from enormous goldfish bowls to elegant single-specimen and delicate, opaque vases.

Terracotta, earthenware and wood

Warm earthenware and terracotta pots also make decorative containers. Because terracotta is porous, however, it will be necessary to line the container with plastic. Wooden containers also need to be lined in this way. Their rustic quality serves as a suitable companion to simple country flowers, making them just right for informal cottage-garden arrangements.

CHAPTER THREE

FRESH FLOWERS FOR SPECIAL OCCASIONS

Hardly a week of the year goes by without some sort of special occasion. It may be a friend's birthday, a wedding anniversary, or a simple luncheon. Then there are all the holidays such as Christmas, Easter, and Thanksgiving and, of course, weddings. Flowers play an important part in all these festivities; they have been used as symbols of celebration through the ages by people from every country in the world. Whether the occasion is formal or informal, there is nothing like flowers for making us feel welcome.

It is a good idea to keep the flower displays for special occasions very seasonal. Now that it is possible to buy a wide range of flowers throughout the year, it is important to be selective and to choose flowers that suit the season as closely as possible.

Arrangements for Valentine's Day
Red roses are the traditional Valentine's Day gift, but the arrangements here use them in more unusual ways. A single rose among delicate white and cream flowers (left) is always striking, while the basket arrangement mixes miniature roses with sprigs of fern and frothy gypsophila sprays.

Bouquets and nosegays

Flowers make an excellent present for every occasion. Every flower contains a message of transformation and growth, of joy and sunshine. Whether a pretty nosegay of flowers from the garden or assembled by a florist or an extravagant bouquet, a gift of flowers always gives immense pleasure. The very impermanence of flowers makes them all the more precious, a happy experience to remember.

Nosegays for gifts

A nosegay, or all-around bunch of flowers, decorated with a bow makes an ideal present for a simple occasion. You might give a nosegay to your host or hostess at a lunch, coffee or tea party, or to say thank you for a helping hand, or to cheer up someone. A nosegay is an ideal way to say, "I am thinking about you" and makes a lovely gift for a child to offer.

Children's nosegays
Small nosegays of flowers are perfect gifts for children to give. Using scented flowers is a delightful idea.

Spring present
(above)
The delicacy of this mixture of pale pink broom, hyacinths and white anemones is heightened by the dramatic red bow.

Summer tribute
(above)
Poppies are magical, especially when fully open. Here they are mixed with gypsophila.

Another spring gift (left)
The paperwhites and soleil d'or narcissus are deliciously sweet.

Fragrant nosegay
(below)
*A delightful mixed bunch,
composed of scented
peach roses and cream
freesias, together with
pink cornflowers,
variegated privet and
eucalyptus.*

Arranging a nosegay
(above)
*It is often a simple
matter to arrange a
nosegay. When laid open
on its side, the flowers
almost arrange
themselves. You could
also arrange the flowers
separately, perhaps
dividing them by color.*

Bear in mind the language of flowers and give a nosegay that has special meaning. It adds a special charm and, since many of the meanings attributed to flowers are joyful, it is easy to find flowers to do the talking for you. Give a red rose to say, "I love you", daisies for "innocence", some honeysuckle for "devoted affection", some ivy for "fidelity", some tulips for "fame" and hazel catkins for "reconciliation". To make the present and the message last a little longer all the recipient need do is put the whole nosegay into a pitcher or vase.

Bouquets for giving
Whether they contain one sort of flower or a pretty mix of flowers and foliage, bouquets are usually simple to make and always a pleasure to receive. A bouquet is the perfect gift to take to a friend who has invited you for lunch or dinner, or for a neighbor who is ill or who has done you a favor. A bouquet also makes a lovely birthday or anniversary gift, especially if the flowers chosen convey a special meaning.

Although many bouquets are easy to make, it is important not simply to bunch

1 *Begin to create this fan-shaped bouquet with three fronds of fern, the tallest in the center. Set two single chrysanthemums on top of the middle fern so that the flower-heads sit just below the top of it. Place slightly shorter-stemmed Peruvian lilies on either side of the single chrysanthemums.*

Summer bouquet
The warm, complementary tones of the flowers – chrysanthemums, carnations, gerbera, Peruvian lilies and gypsophila – are cooled by the refreshing greens of kerria foliage and fern fronds.

together any flowers that happen to be to hand. Consider carefully your choice of flowers, making sure that the colors combine happily, and include some scented flowers to make it even more pleasurable to receive. Freesias, pinks and sweet-smelling roses can all look lovely in bouquets. If you have none to pick in your garden, you can always buy them from your local flower shop. And make a point of trying to use some unusual forms and textures when combining several kinds of flower and foliage in your bouquet.

A bouquet can be any size you choose, ranging from a small bouquet of freesias and gypsophila or one composed of pinks and some silvery foliage, to a much grander bouquet of lilies, spray carnations and chrysanthemums. Always make the character of the recipient and the nature of the occasion your guide.

Once removed from its wrapping, the bouquet can be either arranged in a single vase, or split up and transformed into several smaller arrangements to be used in various rooms around the house.

3 *Continue layering the flowers, offsetting the shapes, colors and textures as you work down the bouquet. Where the stems overlap – usually about a sixth of the way up – tie a narrow ribbon, and, to finish, attach a complementary bow (see p. 153).*

3

2 *Keeping the longest stems roughly at the center of the bouquet, add some of the larger-flowered gerbera, the carnations and the kerria foliage. Make sure the shape is even. Place a layer of light, airy gypsophila over and around the flowers.*

Entertaining with flowers

To make good food that much more delicious, simply add flowers, not only as decoration for the table, breakfast tray, or picnic blanket, but also to garnish any sort of dish, from salads and sandwiches to fish and fruit, and from cakes and confections to meat and vegetables. A single rose or a few flowers arranged in a vase can make a simple meal seem a little bit special. Likewise, the ritual Sunday morning breakfast in bed with the papers is brightened no end by the addition of a few flowers on the breakfast tray, even if you have to put them there yourself! Of course, it is even better when the flowers – and the breakfast – arrive as a surprise.

Whether you are planning a lunch for friends, a Sunday roast for eight, a romantic dinner for two, or a grand dinner party, make sure you include an arrangement or two to help create a relaxed atmosphere.

Arrangements for such occasions need not be elaborate. In fact, a single flower would make the perfect table centerpiece at the dinner for two. Reflect some of the colors of the room, tablecloth or napkins, even the colors of the food, in the flowers you choose, and try using some fruit or vegetables in the arrangement. Cherries, blackberries, strawberries, curly kale, cabbage leaves and sprigs of herbs can all look absolutely beautiful amongst flowers.

For a candlelit dinner under the night sky, try scented white flowers. A summer picnic demands a crock of brilliant blooms whose colors sing out loud. The vivid reds and yellows of tropical flowers would match an exotic dinner in a greenhouse setting.

Facing arrangement for a sideboard
This mixture of fruits, vegetables and flowers would make a sumptuous arrangement for a dinner party. Grapes, vines and fig leaves, mulberries, blackberries. nectarines, pineapple, runner beans, ornamental cabbage leaves, crab apples, pears and dahlias combine in a memorable celebration of plenty.

Nasturtium and lettuce salad
(above)
*Nasturtium flowers have a tangy
taste like watercress and their
bright colour is perfectly set off by
the pale green lettuce. Pot
marigold, dandelion and pink
runner-bean flowers are an
inedible decoration. This is ideal
served with a walnut oil dressing.*

Endive and herb salad (left)
*A delicious mix of cool colors, this
salad has a base of endive with the
edible flowers of fennel and young
chives added as decoration. Serve
with a lime dressing.*

Flowers with food

Many flowers are good to eat, and it is
undoubtedly true that the more beautiful a
dish looks, the more delicious it tastes.
There are plenty of edible flowers that can
be added to salads. The startling red, orange
and yellow flowers of tasty nasturtiums
make a strong visual impact when set
against the bright greens of lettuce or dark
greens of spinach, pale endive or frilly
chicory. Sweet-scented rose petals, pot
marigolds, violets, primroses, fruit tree
blossoms and the flowers of many herbs all
make beautiful garnishes to a dish.

Mother's Day

Mother's Day is a special occasion when flowers make a lovely gift. Giving a present for Mother's Day is a relatively new tradition, but of all the presents to choose from, flowers are the most popular. On this occasion, it is nice to give flowers that convey a message; as many of the meanings from the language of flowers are to do with the pleasant things of life, it is not difficult to find a combination of flowers that look beautiful together, and at the same time convey some feelings about your relationship with your mother.

You could make a bouquet of roses, meaning "love", with stocks for "lasting beauty" and gillyflowers for "bonds of affection". Or you could combine yellow lilies, meaning "gaiety", with bright red chrysanthemums for "I love" and daffodils for "regard". Other appropriate flowers are bluebells, meaning "constancy", and red tulips as a "declaration of love".

Both bouquets and arrangements of flowers make popular presents and in each case the presentation is all important. A bouquet needs to be crisply wrapped in cellophane with a bow that matches the flowers, while an arrangement should be carefully prepared with an eye on its composition, and prettily beribboned.

Flowers with a message
This pretty basket makes a perfect Mother's Day gift. The white roses are a sign of love while daisies are a symbol of patience. White irises, meaning "message", complete the delightful arrangement.

Easter

The most important festival in the Christian calendar is Easter. At this time of year the churches are decorated with arrangements of lilies, with their great white trumpets and soft, sweet scent. To decorate your home, and for a festive change, make a flowery Easter nest using the seasonal flowers available in your garden and some hand-painted eggs, the traditional symbol of rebirth and renewal.

Making an Easter nest

1 *Cut a rectangle from a piece of chicken wire using wire cutters. Then fold and tuck in the corners to form a nest shape.*

2 *Thread a long wire needle with raffia and sew clumps of hay and alder twigs on to the wire frame to make the nest.*

3 *Line the nest with a waterproof container and then fill with wet foam. Arrange the flowers and eggs in the foam.*

Easter celebration
The completed nest displays a mixture of glowing yellow, pink and fresh green flowers and foliage surrounding a cluster of hand-painted eggs that echo those colors. Any combination of simple flowers can be used to achieve the informal look. This arrangement uses Cape cowslips, flowering-currant twigs, the single chrysanthemum 'Tuneful', the primrose 'Pacific Hybrid' and tiny orchids.

Weddings

The wedding ceremony is one of the most important ceremonies of our lives and because of this the event can be rather overwhelming. However, amid all the formality of the occasion, flowers can provide a welcome element. So it is well worth making that extra effort to create beautiful arrangements.

The bride usually carries a bouquet of flowers, and this can take a variety of forms, ranging from a simple bunch of garden flowers to a much more elaborate bouquet where the flowers are wired so that they can overflow in a delicate shower of blooms and foliage. The style and colors of the flowers used depend on the type of wedding and the design of the bride's dress. A bunch of lilies can make an elegant bouquet to be carried in the crook of the arm, or, for a more informal wedding, a simple nosegay can be just right.

Then there are the flowers for the bride's hair. Again, they can be simple, single flowers or a circlet or half-circlet of flowers that garland her head.

Bridesmaids, too, usually carry flowers. They can be similar to those the bride carries, although it is more usual for bridesmaids to carry small nosegays rather than a shower bouquet. If they are small children, they can carry little baskets or small hoops of flowers, or maybe even a pretty ball of flowers hanging from a ribbon. The bridesmaids' flowers should complement the color and style of their dresses, and relate to the bride's flowers.

Boutonnieres
(right and below)
Traditional and more unusual decorations for groom and guests:
1 orchid – a favorite flower for weddings – with camellia leaves;
2 peach rose with eucalyptus leaves;
3 a simple white rose.
(See pp. 189–90 for wiring flower stems.)

1

2

3

Flowery comb for a bridesmaid (above and top)
Assemble three small bunches of your chosen flowers and foliage (see pp. 189–90 for wiring). Cover the wire with floral tape and then wire one bunch of flowers to the comb, covering the tie with tape. Wire on the other two bunches to overlap the first. Leave 1 inch of wire at each end in order to secure the decoration to the comb by twisting the ends between the teeth.

Making the bride's bouquet

1 *Wire all the ingredients individually to strengthen and lengthen stems (see pp. 189–90).*

2 *Begin making the trail by binding some ferns, flowers and foliage together with reel wire.*

3 *Wire in more flowers one by one to establish the triangular shape of the trail.*

4 *Cover the wire with floral tape as you go. Complete the trail by bending the stems below the flowers.*

5 *Add the remaining material above the trail, binding the wires near the bend. Spread the flowers.*

6 *Leaving ends to trail, wrap ribbon around the handle. Tie the ends and add a bow (see p. 153).*

Trailing bouquet for a bride
Although this bouquet is time-consuming to make, the end result looks sumptuous with its sparkling white flowers and silver and green leaves; it also has a delightful, fresh scent. The flowers and foliage used are lilies-of-the-valley, heather sprigs, orchids, stephanotis flowers, rosemary sprigs, ivy, larkspur, senecio, white roses and fern fronds.

Preparing wedding flowers

All the flowers that are carried or worn at a wedding have to be prepared only a short while before the ceremony as they will soon begin to wilt. Before arranging them, it is best to give them a good, long drink of water. Carnations and spray carnations, single chrysanthemums, freesias, Peruvian lilies, stephanotis, gypsophila and half-open roses all last quite well and can be prepared up to 12 hours in advance, so long as they are then kept in a cool place. It is not a good idea to keep them in the refrigerator, however, as this is *too* cold and the flowers can easily become frosted. Sweet peas, full blown roses, Christmas roses and lilies-of-the-valley are more short-lived.

Flowers for the church

Just as important as the flowers for the bride, bridesmaids and guests are the flowers that decorate the church. It looks lovely if these can echo the colors of the bride's flowers, but bear in mind that churches are brightly lit. Often very pale or very bright flower arrangements look best.

There are usually two substantial flower arrangements made for inside the church, one on either side of the altar, that can be seen from every position. It is also a nice idea to have an arrangement near the entrance to welcome everyone. Window sills can also be decorated, pillars can be garlanded and arrangements can also be made for the pew ends.

Flower sphere (below)
This pretty ball on long, pink ribbons is a charming mixture of tiny cream and pink roses, smilax and laurustinus. To prepare the base, soak a foam sphere (see below left) in water. Double over a piece of heavy gauge stem wire and push it through the sphere, leaving a wire loop sticking out of the foam. Bend the two ends back and secure to the loop. Thread a ribbon through the loop, tie the ends together and hang the ball up. Stud the foam with flowers and foliage to cover and finally attach a bow to the ribbon.

Flower basket
(above)
A basket of delicate little flowers looks very pretty and is easy for a young bridesmaid to carry. The colors of the flowers should complement the color of her dress. This arrangement uses miniature cream and pink roses, statice, leather fern and heather.

Base for flower sphere

Pew end for special guests

Pew ends provide a glowing welcome. These flowers will last well because they are secured in wet foam. The arrangement is comprised of decorative cabbage, speciosum lily, montbretia, Michaelmas daisies, fennel, barberry, larkspur, yellow roses and beech foliage. Bouquets could also be hung, but they would have to be made at the last minute to ensure that they look fresh throughout the ceremony.

Making a pew end

1 *Fill the hanging frame with foam, dampened and trimmed to fit. Then affix the cabbage into the central compartment on top of the frame.*

2 *Insert the shorter flowers around the cabbage, filling in at the back. Add the taller lily, montbretia and foliage to form the trail.*

Harvest time and Thanksgiving

With autumn comes the ripening of many crops: grains, apples, pears, pomegranates, persimmons and melons, nuts and grapes, artichokes and Indian corn, pumpkins and multicolored peppers. Homes are filled with the fruits of the harvest: even those in the cities manage to have wondrous displays of gold and rust and yellow. These colors are echoed by the many varieties of chrysanthemum and dahlia, strawflower and gladioli that flower in profusion at this wonderful time of year.

The celebration of the harvest is one of the most ancient of all festivals, dating from pagan times when communities were dependent on the success of their own crops. Today, we are not nearly so aware of the quality of the harvest. Even after a very wet and sunless summer, when the farmers have been complaining that the harvest will be poor, there are still bountiful supplies of harvest fruits and vegetables in the markets.

Harvest and Thanksgiving are traditional times to celebrate and to reflect on the effects of the seasons on our lives. What better way to do this than to give a Thanksgiving party with harvest decorations. Arrangements look splendid in glowing autumn colors: rich amber, sunny gold and nutty brown. Make the fruits, vegetables and grains an integral part of your harvest arrangement, perhaps created for a Thanksgiving table display, or incorporate them in a garland to be placed around a doorway or buffet table.

Autumnal celebration
A small, hollowed-out pumpkin lined with plastic forms the container for this arrangement. The late sunshine colors make this a happy combination of spindle, snowberries, Chinese lanterns, and strawflowers.

Seasonal garland

Garlands are a lovely way of decorating a door, fireplace, table, niche or painting. If you wish to make a long garland, join together individual moss-filled chicken wire tubes with mossing wire, and cover with more wired plant material. This one is decorated with 'Destiny' lilies, rose hips, lady apples, red and yellow peppers, chilli peppers, box foliage, barley, old man's beard and eucalyptus.

Making a robust garland

1 *Decide how long your garland is to be and make the appropriate number of chicken wire tubes (see p. 183). Join them with spool wire. Then wire the peppers, apples (see p. 171) and lilies (see p. 190).*

2 *Taking one section of tube at a time, poke the stems and wires of the ingredients into the moss. The flowers must lie in the direction in which the garland will hang. Overlap the material to hide the base.*

Christmas

The countdown to Christmas Day begins the month before with the four weeks of Advent. In many countries this period is celebrated with a wreath containing four candles, one being lit on each Sunday of the month. You can make an Advent wreath with fresh flowers and foliage and renew it each week. Even at the beginning of Advent the decorations are in evidence for Christmas. More entertaining is done at this season than at any other time of year and there are many opportunities for wonderful arrangements.

There has been a midwinter festival since early pagan times, when boughs of evergreen, including mistletoe, conifer, holly and ivy, were brought into the house. In the fourth century, Christmas – the word is derived from Christ's Mass – was first celebrated by the Church and gradually the pagan and Christian festivals became merged. The exchanging of presents was a pre-Christian tradition; so too was the custom of having lanterns in the house, which today take the form of Christmas tree lights. The Christmas tree is quite a recent addition to the celebrations, made popular by Prince Albert, who imported large numbers of them from his estate in Coburg in 1845. Flowers and evergreen foliage now play a large part in our Christmas festivities. Christmas trees are sold in their millions and it is exciting to decorate the house with some beautiful flower arrangements and garlanding. Flower shops can supply a wide range of colorful and long-lasting flowers, as well as the familiar holly, mistletoe, ivy and pine tree branches.

The more traditional Christmas arrangements and decorations are always appreciated: a Christmas tree simply decorated a few days before Christmas with lights and bows; a wreath of holly and pine for the front door; some rich garlanding; and some arrangements in glowing colors, perhaps with candles, to brighten the hallway, living room, sideboard or the dinner table. They are part of the magic of Christmas.

Traditional circular wreath
Variegated holly and blue spruce are attached to a frame (see p. 183) and decorated with satin balls and bow.

Pine spray
Three branches of blue spruce are hung with cones, baubles and raffia strands and twists.

Christmas party centerpiece
A useful white ceramic Lazy Susan creates the structure for this cascading arrangement. Brilliant red and green keynotes are established with red roses and vigorous butcher's-broom foliage. Rowan clusters, snowberries and green candles develop the theme.

Christmas garlands

Of the three different types of garlanding shown here, the robust garland would look best against a wall, maybe surrounding a mirror or window. The delicate garland would be ideal for a shelf, mantelpiece or around a painting, and the traditional swag would look good adorning a large fireplace in a living room.

Traditional garland

1 *Arrange fir branches bearing cones, overlapping them to make the shape you want to create. Tie the branches together in several places, making sure that they are held together very securely.*

2 *Fill out the garland by tying in pieces of berried holly and elaeagnus along the whole length.*

Delicate garland

Braid strands of raffia to the length you require (see p. 185). Then thread groups of gold-sprayed butcher's-broom leaves and silver-sprayed larch cone twigs into the braid at regular intervals. For an even more festive look, add wired gold balls into each clump of plant material.

Robust garland

Chicken wire stuffed with moss (see
p. 183) forms the basis of this swag.
Push or wire evergreen sprigs
into the frame and then thread
wired fruits into the moss base.
Add the artificial cherries last.

DRIED
FLOWERS

———

Chapter Four

Guide to Dried Flowers and Foliage

The following pages are a color-by-color guide to the dried flowers and plants that make the ingredients of arrangements. Some plants, such as statice (*Limonium* sp.), roses (*Rosa* sp.) and everlasting flowers (*Helichrysum* sp.), are invaluable since they grow in a profusion of different forms and colors.

The ingredients illustrated are widely available, although they originate from many regions of the world. A few of them (some cones and leaves) were gathered from the wild with great care, so as not to damage the parent plant. Always check before you pick whether the material is a protected or endangered species and never take any wild plant material that falls into this category. Ask the landowner's permission before picking anything under cultivation.

Natural riches
An array of dried flowers hanging on a wall has as much visual interest as a rich rug or tapestry. The abundant mixture of colors and textures in these bunches of roses, helipterum, strawflowers, yarrow, physalis, statice and barley complements the rustic feel of the whitewashed wall.

Reds and pinks

Pink fescue grass
Festuca sp.

Honesty
Lunaria rediviva

Brome grass
Bromus sp.

Pink cardoon
Cynara sp.

Onion
Allium sp.

Hair-grass
Aira sp.

Protea
Protea compacta

Pennisetum
Pennisetum sp.

**Pale pink
fescue grass**
Festuca sp.

Protea
Banksia occidentalis

Common quaking grass
Briza media

Protea
*Banksia
menziesii*

Peony
*Paeonia
lactiflora*

Hydrangea
Hydrangea macrophylla

Hair-grass
Aira sp.

Larkspur
Consolida sp.

**Pink-tinged
hybrid tea rose**
Rosa 'Gerda'

Rhodanthe
Helipterum manglesii

Acroclinium
Helipterum roseum

**Vermilion
floribunda rose**
Rosa cv.

Peach everlasting
or **strawflower**
Helichrysum bracteatum

Campion
Silene sp.

Red bottlebrush
Callistemon beaufortia sparsa

**Cerise-tinged
hybrid tea rose**
Rosa 'Mercedes'

Salmon-pink statice
Limonium sp.

Acroclinium
Helipterum sp.

**Terracotta
miniature rose**
Rosa cv.

Globe amaranth
Gomphrena globosa

Silver strawberry
Leptospermum sp.

Phaenocoma shrub
Phaenocoma prolifera

Rich red everlasting
or **strawflower**
Helichrysum
bracteatum

Bell heather
Erica cinerea

Gayfeather
Liatris spicata

Deep scarlet
hybrid tea rose
Rosa 'Ilona'

Russian or **rat's tail statice**
Limonium suworowii

Celastrus
Celastrus sp.

Copper beech
Fagus sylvatica 'Cuprea'

Deep red everlasting
or **strawflower**
*Helichrysum
bracteatum*

Yarrow
Achillea millefolium

Pom-pom dahlia
Dahlia sp.

**Scarlet-tinged
hybrid tea rose**
Rosa 'Jaguar'

Celosia cockscomb
Celosia argentea cristata

**Red
kangaroo paw**
*Anigozanthos
rufus*

Leucodendron
Leucodendron sp.

Bronze-leaved eucalyptus
Eucalyptus sp.

Oranges and yellows

Cluster-flowered everlasting or **strawflower**
Helichrysum italicum

Pale yellow everlasting or **strawflower**
Helichrysum sp.

Curry plant
Helichrysum angustifolium

Deep yellow hybrid tea rose
Rosa 'Golden Times'

Craspedia
Craspedia globosa

**Golden
everlasting** or **strawflower**
Helichrysum sp.

Deep yellow yarrow
Achillea filipendulina
'Coronation Gold'

Sunray
Helipterum sp.

**Bronze-tinged
hybrid tea rose**
Rosa 'La Minuette'

Yellow kangaroo paw
Anigozanthos sp.

**Silver-leaved
everlasting** or **strawflower**
Helichrysum sp.

Chrysanthemum
Chrysanthemum sp.

Protea
Banksia baxteri

Lady's mantle
Alchemilla mollis

African daisies
Arctosis sp.

Mimosa
Acacia sp.

Jerusalem sage
Phlomis fruticosa

**Golden-flowered
statice**
Limonium sp.

Goldenrod
Solidago canadensis

Golden yarrow
Achillea sp.

Feather flower
Verticordia sp.

Dryandra
Dryandra quercifolia

Protea
Banksia attenuata

Light golden yarrow
Achillea sp.

Deep salmon-pink statice
Limonium sp.

Chinese lantern
Physalis alkekengi franchetii

Decorative corn (fruit)
Zea mays

Chrysanthemum
Chrysanthemum sp.

Chrysanthemum
Chrysanthemum vulgare

Buttercup
Ranunculus sp.

Chinese lantern
Physalis alkekengi franchetii

Dock
Rumex sp.

Pot marigold
Calendula officinalis

Safflower or dyer's saffron
Carthamus tinctorius

**Orange-yellow
hybrid tea rose**
Rosa cv.

Small-headed yarrow
Achillea sp.

Greens and browns

Pin oak
Quercus palustris

Clubrush
Scirpus sp.

Lesser or **small
quaking grass**
Briza minima

Big or **large
quaking grass**
Briza maxima

Linden
Tilia sp.

Dill
*Anethum
graveolens*

Bamboo
Arundinaria sp.

Protea
Banksia sp.

Six-rowed barley
Hordeum vulgare

Timothy
*Phleum
pratense*

Big or **large
quaking grass**
Briza maxima

Hydrangea
*Hydrangea
paniculata*

Hydrangea
*Hydrangea
macrophylla*

Ribbon grass
Phalaris arundinacea

**Rough
bristle
grass**
*Setaria
verticillata*

Ivy
Hedera helix

Cup plant
Hakea cucullata

Fringe myrtle
Calytrix sp.

Male fern
Dryopteris filix-mas

Alyssum
Alyssum sp.

Cress
Capsella sp.

Moss
Mnium sp.

Beech
Fagus sylvatica

Mignonette
Reseda lutea

Bamboo
Arundinaria sp.

Grevillea
Grevillea sp.

Chenopodium
Chenopodium sp.

Clubmoss
Selaginella sp.

Love-in-a-mist
Nigella damascena

Goldenrod
Solidago canadensis 'Lemore'

Grimmia moss or **bun moss**
Grimmia pulvinata

Love-lies-bleeding
Amaranthus caudatus 'Viridis'

Snow gum
Eucalyptus niphophila

Scots pine
Pinus sylvestris

Rush
Juncus sp.

Hydrangea
Hydrangea macrophylla

Leucodendron
Leucodendron sp.

Dryandra
Dryandra sp.

Reed
Phragmites australis

Bamboo
Arundinaria sp.

Leucodendron
Leucodendron stelligerum

Clubrush
Scirpus sp.

**Lemon-scented
bottlebrush**
*Callistemon
citrinus*

**Mexican
orange blossom**
Choisya ternata

Hakea
Hakea sp.

Reed
Phragmites australis

Pine cone
Pinus sp.

Black-eared barley
Hordeum sp.

Rattan palm or **wait-awhile vine**
Calamus sp.

Paradise nut or **sapucia nut**
Lecythis usitata

Cattails
Typha angustifolia

Top-brush
Leucodendron rubrum

Mugwort
Artemisia vulgaris

Scots pine cone
Pinus sylvestris

Mexican white pine cone
Pinus ayacahuite

Larch cone
Larix sp.

Pin oak
Quercus palustris

Cattails
Typha latifolia

Lotus pods (fruit)
Nelumbo lucifera

Reed
Phragmites australis

Silver birch
Betula pendula

Millet
Milium sp.

Globe artichoke
Cynara scolymus

Love-in-a-mist
Nigella damascena

Ornamental onion
Allium aflatunense

Hop
Humulus lupulus

Egyptian paper rush or **papyrus**
Cyperus papyrus

Fescue grass
Festuca sp.

Sedge
Carex sp.

Leucodendron
Leucodendron sp.

Physocarpus
Physocarpus sp.

Blues and purples

Lavender
Lavandula spica

Larkspur
Delphinium consolida

Globe thistle
Echinops ritro

**Large-flowered
sea lavender**
Limonium sp.

**Miniature globe
thistle**
Echinops ritro

Hydrangea
Hydrangea macrophylla
'Générale Vicomtesse de Vibraye'

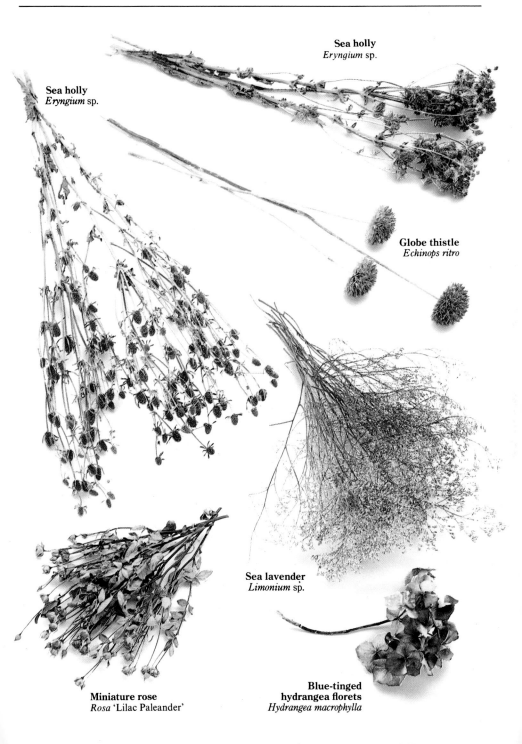

Sea holly
Eryngium sp.

Sea holly
Eryngium sp.

Globe thistle
Echinops ritro

Sea lavender
Limonium sp.

Miniature rose
Rosa 'Lilac Paleander'

**Blue-tinged
hydrangea florets**
Hydrangea macrophylla

Mauve statice
Limonium sinuatum

Perennial delphinium
Delphinium elatum cv.

Monkshood
Aconitum napellus

Astilbe
Astilbe davidii

Love-lies-bleeding
Amaranthus sp.

Cornflower
Centaurea cyanus

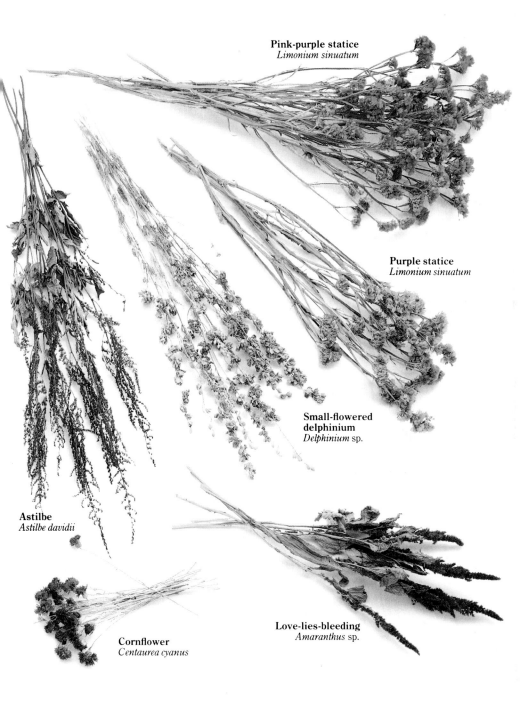

Pink-purple statice
Limonium sinuatum

Purple statice
Limonium sinuatum

**Small-flowered
delphinium**
Delphinium sp.

Astilbe
Astilbe davidii

Cornflower
Centaurea cyanus

Love-lies-bleeding
Amaranthus sp.

Whites, creams, silvers

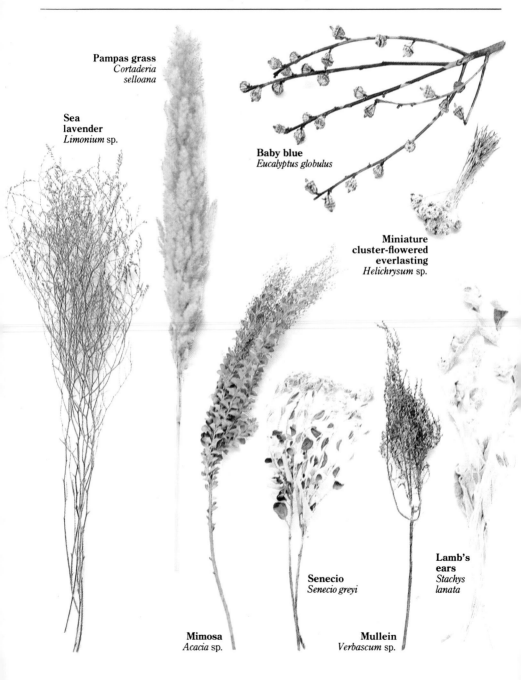

Pampas grass
*Cortaderia
selloana*

**Sea
lavender**
Limonium sp.

Baby blue
Eucalyptus globulus

**Miniature
cluster-flowered
everlasting**
Helichrysum sp.

Senecio
Senecio greyi

**Lamb's
ears**
*Stachys
lanata*

Mimosa
Acacia sp.

Mullein
Verbascum sp.

Melaleuca
Melaleuca sp.

Daisy bush
Olearia sp.

Silver-flowered everlasting
Cephalipterum drummondii

Stirlingia
Stirlingia latifolia

Miniature cluster-flowered everlasting
Helichrysum sp.

Everlasting silver foliage
Helichrysum sp.

Miniature everlasting
Pithocarpa corymbulosa

Chamomile
Anthemis nobilis

Bupleurum
Bupleurum sp.

Baby's breath
Gypsophila sp.

**Silver
everlasting** or **strawflower**
Helichrysum sp.

Dgingarra leaf
Kingia australis

Helipterum
*Helipterum
manglesii*

Helipterum
Helipterum sp.

**Silky
serruria**
Serruria sp.

Seacrest
*Helichrysum
cordatum*

**Cream
delphinium**
Delphinium sp.

Lachnostachys
Lachnostachys sp.

Miniature helipterum
Helipterum sp.

Sea lavender
Limonium sp.

White delphinium
Delphinium sp.

Cream statice
Limonium sp.

Sandflower
or **winged everlasting**
Ammobium sp.

**Australian
daisy**
Ixodia sp.

Cotton
*Gossypium
herbaceum*

**Willow-
myrtle**
*Agonis
juniperina*

**Pampas
grass**
*Cortaderia
selloana*

Bear's breeches
Acanthus spinosus

Woody pear
Xylomelum angustifolium

Pink fruits
Dianthus sp.

Hosta (fruit)
Hosta sp.

Stemless thistle
Carlina acaulis
'Caulescens'

Hydrangea
*Hydrangea
macrophylla*

Strawflower
*Helichrysum
bracteatum*

Lapsana
Lapsana sp.

Bells of Ireland
or **shell flower**
Moluccella laevis

**White-flowering
hybrid tea rose**
Rosa
'Jack Frost'

Sphagnum moss
Sphagnum sp.

Onion
Allium sp.

Heracleum
Heracleum sphondylium

Chenopodium
Chenopodium sp.

Field poppy (fruit)
Papaver rhoeas

Feather flower
Verticordia sp.

Pampas grass
Cortaderia selloana

Tassel flower
Cacalia sp.

Cluster-flowered helipterum
Helipterum sp.

Grass daisy
Aphyllanthes sp.

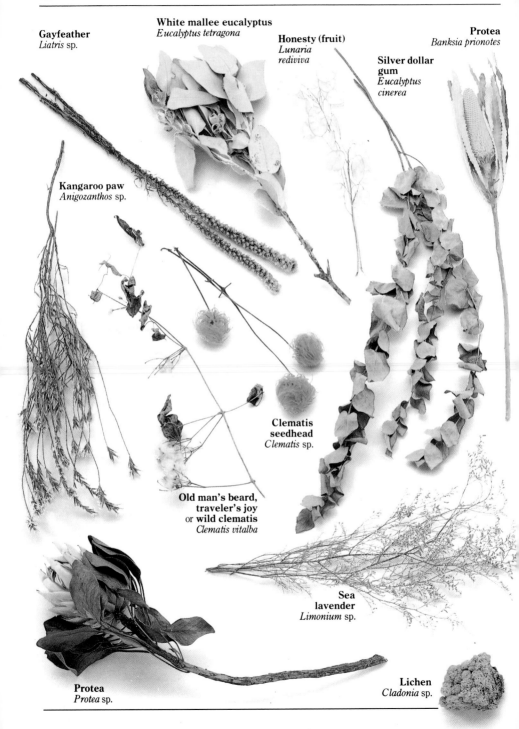

Gayfeather
Liatris sp.

White mallee eucalyptus
Eucalyptus tetragona

Honesty (fruit)
*Lunaria
rediviva*

**Silver dollar
gum**
*Eucalyptus
cinerea*

Protea
Banksia prionotes

Kangaroo paw
Anigozanthos sp.

**Clematis
seedhead**
Clematis sp.

**Old man's beard,
traveler's joy
or wild clematis**
Clematis vitalba

**Sea
lavender**
Limonium sp.

Lichen
Cladonia sp.

Protea
Protea sp.

Additional dried plant material

The dried plant material illustrated on the previous pages according to color is not an exhaustive guide to the wealth of material available. The table below lists a further selection of flowers and foliage that can be used successfully in dried arrangements, with an at-a-glance color reference to the variety of shades available, to enable you to plan your arrangements effectively.

	REDS	PINKS	ORANGES	YELLOWS	BROWNS	GREENS	BLUES	PURPLES	WHITES	CREAMS	SILVERS
Allium afflatunense Decorative onion		•									
Alstroemeria ligtu Peruvian lily	•	•	•	•				•			
Amaryllis belladonna Belladonna lily	•	•						•			
Anaphalis margaritacea Pearly everlasting								•			
Anemone coronaria Anemone, windflower	•	•		•		•	•	•			
Astilbe arendsii Astilbe, goat's beard		•			•				•		
Bupleurum sp. Bupleurum						•		•			
Camellia japonica Camellia	•	•				•					
Centaurea macrocephala Large-headed centaurea				•							
Choisya ternata Mexican orange blossom								•			
Corylus avallana contorta Walking stick					•						
Cytisus scoparius (Scotch) Broom		•		•		•		•			
Dahlia sp. Pom-pom dahlia	•		•	•			•	•			
Delphinium ajacis Larkspur		•					•	•	•		
Elaeagnus pungens Elaeagnus						•					
Eucalyptus ficifolia Flowering gum					•	•					
Gentiana sino-ornata Gentian							•				
Gomphrena globosa Globe amaranth								•			
Helleborus sp. Christmas rose, Lenten rose		•				•		•			
Iris foetidissima Stinking iris	•										
Kochia sp.	•					•					•
Lilium sp. Lily		•	•	•				•			
Magnolia sp. Magnolia		•						•			
Mahonia japonica Mahonia				•		•					
Picea pungens glauca Silver spruce											•
Polygonatum multiflorum Solomon's seal								•			
Salvia sp. Sage							•	•			
Santolina sp. Lavender cotton				•							•
Sedum spectabile Spectacular sedum		•									
Verticordia nitens Golden morrison				•							
Xanthorrhoea sp. Glass tree spears					•						
Xeranthemum sp. Immortelle							•	•			
Zinnia elegans Zinnia	•		•	•					•		

· CHAPTER FIVE ·

PRINCIPLES OF DRIED FLOWER ARRANGING

Nature is the best guide when creating
arrangements of dried flowers. There
are no hard and fast rules. Plant shapes
are well balanced and attractive when
viewed singly or in groups. These are
the shapes and groupings to bear
in mind when creating arrangements.
Before choosing your plant material or
container, or deciding on the shape of
the arrangements, it is best to consider
the position the arrangement will take.
How large does it need to be? Will it be
seen from all sides? What sort of
background will it be seen against?
The container is also important.
Natural and simple containers are
usually suitable and often the shape
and texture of the container will
suggest shapes and textures for the
arrangement. Dried flowers with
warm, glowing colors look sumptuous
in copper, brass and terracotta
containers, whereas cool white and
pale-colored flowers look very
attractive in silver and
stone containers.

Complementary container
*This mix of many of the tones in the blue and purple
range complements the spiral of blue and turquoise
that twists down the trumpet-shaped vase. The
flowers in this striking and rich arrangement include
echinops, sea holly, statice and larkspur.*

Style

Every arrangement of flowers – whether for a garland or a vase – contains a number of design elements which together create a certain style. The shape, color and texture of the arrangement, together with the container if there is one and the situation in which the finished arrangement is placed, combine to give a total "look" or style.

The informality of dried flowers
Dried flowers have a natural and informal style of their own and however formal a shape you create, the completed arrangement will always have a sense of informality about it for the natural style of the flowers should greatly influence the style of the arrangement.

Simple arrangement for a bedroom table
This delicate trifoliate china dish holds a sea of pale blue delphinium flowers. Sand-dried pink roses and an auratum lily float nonchalantly on top. The complete arrangement is ideal for a romantic bedroom, bringing a touch of summer indoors.

It is often a good idea to emphasize the informal nature of dried flowers, and some of the most successful dried-flower arrangements are those that have the informality of a summer garden. Containers with a rustic feel to them work well with such arrangements precisely because they are close to the look of the plants themselves. Baskets of all types, wooden bowls and boxes, terracotta and stoneware bowls, ceramics with less sophisticated designs and finishes, all lend themselves to natural-looking, dried-flower arrangements.

Careful planning
Although a natural-looking arrangement might appear simple to achieve, it actually requires careful planning if it is not to look artificial. To begin with, it needs strength of line: curves must be strong and straight lines must be well defined. For the lines are the bones of the arrangement: they give the arrangement its essential shape. Whether created by the stems, the leaves

or seedheads, or even the flowers themselves, they should be made first and the shape filled out afterwards. In this way the arrangement will be much easier to complete without spoiling the shape.

Cultivating your own style

Each of us has our own sense of style. When we open a magazine or book, certain images, colors and shapes appeal to us and we should draw upon these images when creating a dried-flower arrangement.

It is a good idea to make a note of the plants and colors that appeal to you. When you visit a garden, notice the combinations of flowers and foliage, and the shapes of the trees and shrubs that you like best. Then you can grow some of these plants yourself for drying, or buy bunches of them ready dried if you are not lucky enough to have a garden, and use them to create many different arrangements for your home – all reflecting your own sense of style.

The style of the room

Fortunately, a great many dried-flower arrangements fit in with even the most striking interior designs. The strong shapes of flowers like yarrow, the soft haze of fluffy gypsophila, the stately seedheads of poppies and bulrushes: all these look wonderful against both the steel and glass of a cool, modern room and the warm, mellow wood of an old country house.

However, each room does have its own particular style, which might dictate a certain type of arrangement. The kitchen, a utilitarian place, is the ideal room in which to hang bunches of dried flowers from the ceiling, where they will be out of the way but will still form an attractive and eye-catching arrangement.

In the living room there is usually more space for table arrangements. Where there is a fireplace, a grand arrangement of dried flowers will cover the empty grate very attractively throughout the summer months. The bedroom generally has a softer style and so a gentler, prettier, perhaps more subdued, arrangement will probably be more in tune there.

Suiting the interior (top and above)
A strong yellow wall color (top) inspired the arrangement for this elegant period fireplace throughout the summer. The abundant plant material includes yellow sunray, mimosa, golden yarrow and large-headed centaurea. In contrast, the striking arrangement of bamboo and hydrangea heads (above) complements the shapes and colors in a boldly decorated modern interior.

Color

So much plant material can be preserved that the color palette available to the dried-flower arranger is spectacular, and all the colors can be used in an infinite number of combinations to create a wide range of different effects.

Combining colors

It is a good idea to experiment with different combinations of colors in different quantities when beginning to create dried-flower arrangements, to discover which colors look best together.

In general, colors that lie near each other in the spectrum blend together to create a subdued but none-the-less attractive combination. So, red and orange blend well, likewise orange and yellow, yellow and green, green and blue, and blue and violet. Colors at one remove from each other in the spectrum also combine well, but produce a more striking result.

Using green and red
An eighteenth-century French faience plate is the inspiration for this arrangement of dark roses and their leaves. The addition of a brighter red rose seems to intensify the color in all the flowers. The blue cornflowers echo those on the rim of the plate.

Red contrasts pleasantly with yellow, orange with green, yellow with blue, and green with violet.

In essence, the further apart two colors are from one another the more startling the effect they create. Consequently, combinations of red and green flowers, red and blue flowers, and orange or yellow and violet or purple flowers will create an extremely dramatic effect. In addition, combining a small quantity of one color with a larger amount of an opposing color intensifies the dominant color. For example, a green arrangement appears even greener when a small amount of bright red is added.

Tones and shades

Pastel colors are simply muted tones of primary and secondary colors. If you were creating a pastel color with paint you would add white, the color of light, to the primary or secondary color. Pale pink, peach and apricot, lilac, lemon and pale icy blues are all pastel colors. By adding black, the color of darkness, to a primary or secondary color you would create a more somber tone, such as brown, rust, gray, navy blue or plum.

Pastel tones and shades are especially well represented in dried flowers. There are many pink flowers, ranging from bright to pale, that are extremely easy to dry. (See The Directory of Flowers and Foliage, pages 206–34.)

Choosing colors

By choosing colors that are close to each other in the spectrum you cannot really go wrong. But you will probably create a more interesting arrangement by being a bit more adventurous. Don't be afraid of mixing any colors at all, or indeed using only one color by itself for a bold effect. Finally, consider the impact you wish to make with your finished arrangement. A large centerpiece, for example, will probably require a dramatic use of color.

Blending warm colors (above)
This glowing combination of summer flowers features pink peonies that have been dried chemically. These are offset by red roses, delicate bunches of silene, deeper pink onion heads and acacia foliage.

Muted harmony (below)
An elegant arrangement composed of closely related white, cream and silver tones, including carline thistles, hydrangeas, helichrysum, moluccella, gypsophila and honesty.

Choosing containers

Most dried-flower arrangements require a decorative container – a basket, a vase, a saucer, a dish, or some other receptacle. The choice of container is very important because, in a successful arrangement, container and plant material fuse to create a combined effect that is infinitely greater than that of either the flowers or the container separately. There should be a harmony of scale, shape, color and texture between container and flowers. They should look completely natural together, as though they had always been meant for each other.

The scope for choosing containers is enormous. They need not be expensive nor need they be watertight. In fact, your home is probably full of containers that you have never thought of as being suitable for dried flower arrangements.

It is a good idea to make a collection of any containers that appeal to you, whatever their shape or size, but bear in mind that it is easier to make arrangements in containers with necks that are a little smaller than their bodies.

The less decorative a container, the bigger the variety of dried flowers you can use without the flowers clashing with the container. Since glass, metal and terracotta containers tend to be less decorative than ceramic ones, they open up a wider range of dried material for use.

The range of container materials

You should be able to find some glass containers in the kitchen – a tumbler, a pitcher or a bowl, for instance. All glass containers need to be lined with moss, petals or leaves, as the stems of dried flowers are not as attractive as those of their fresh counterparts.

Simple rectangular, square or cylindrical clear glass containers are the easiest to use since they are visually undemanding. Colored glass restricts the choice of flower color and forces you to be more inventive. Most difficult to arrange in is

Eighteenth-century box (left)
The painted paper lining of this container is so beautiful that a section is left showing. That, and the wonderfully subtle colors of the rug, made the choice of the ingredients – oats, fern, strawflowers, globe thistles and larkspur – inevitable. They are arranged informally to accentuate the natural, relaxed atmosphere of the room.

Glass for a sectional arrangement
A smooth glass cylinder exploits differences of texture. Separate portions of cinnamon, dried chestnuts, lentils, pasta, lavender, sunflower seeds and Indian corn are pressed against the glass by moss, while fir cones and poppy and love-in-the-mist seedheads are arranged in segments on top.

sophisticated, highly reflective glass, which, like fine china and porcelain, can demand a formal arrangement.

Wooden containers are particularly useful, as the wood itself combines strongly with the feel of dried flowers. From a wide variety of possibilities, you might choose a curved, olive-wood salad bowl or a small box decorated with inlaid wood. A rough wooden box that seedlings have been grown in can be used for an arrangement that imitates a mossy field or it can be filled with low, brilliantly colored helichrysums, their heads peeping just above its rim. Take advantage of the worn colors of old painted wood or the jewel-like colors of lacquered wood from India or Japan to create some distinctive arrangements. Baskets are also favored for their

natural qualities. You might consider a waste-paper basket, a shopping basket, an old sewing basket, a simple bread basket or, for a floor-standing arrangement, a heavy-weight log basket.

Try cake-pans and molds, worn copper saucepans or iron casseroles, or, at the other end of the scale, perhaps an eighteenth-century silver pitcher or a pewter and brass Art Nouveau vase.

Search out ceramic containers with interesting glazes, such as lustrous metallic, pitted or crystalline. Raid the garden for terracotta pots, especially those with a mossy surface. Terracotta saucers can be transformed into marvelous dried flower gardens. Likely candidates in the kitchen are a casserole dish, a pitcher or mug, a sugar bowl or maybe a teapot, unused because of a broken lid.

The garden is also the most likely source for stone containers such as urns and vases. They look splendid filled with enormous arrangements of dried flowers, the neutral colors of the stone complementing almost any color combination of flowers and foliage.

Wreaths

Many types of arrangement do not need to be set in a container but are made on some sort of framework.

A circular arrangement such as a wreath can be based on either a copper wire frame, purchased ready-made from a flower shop or some general stores, or a chicken wire and moss frame you can build yourself (see p. 183). Alternatively, you can twist grape vines, clematis, honeysuckle or actinidia, or supple twigs such as birch or willow, into a circle (see p. 184), entwining them and working in the ends so the finished frame is firm enough to be used as a base for attaching a variety of dried flowers, should you wish. In fact, if carefully done, such a vine wreath can look beautiful in its own right.

Harvest wreath
(below)
The final effect of the wreath (made in the sequence opposite) suggests the mellow warmth of autumn.

Vine wreath
(right)
Hay bundles, red roses, cornflowers, achillea and xeranthemum are bound on with raffia.

Bound-straw base
(below)
This simple circle comprises pale-pink and cream helichrysum, cornflowers and gypsophila. Generous pink ribbons provide the finishing touch.

Whimsical wreath
(right)
Entwined vines form the base of this wreath, decorated with rose leaves, pine cones and moss. A nest of woven hay, complete with eggs and blue-bird sentinel, nestles in part of the vine weave.

Making a small wreath

1 *Take a dry, prepared moss base (see p. 183). Wire sprigs of hops, flowerheads of ammobium, bunches of oats and single yellow roses. Cover the wired stems with stem-wrap tape (see p. 191).*

2 *Insert the stems of ammobium flowers into the base to provide the background to the wreath design, pushing each wire through the moss and bending it back into the base behind the wreath.*

3 *Choose the hanging point of the wreath and then complete the arrangement by filling in the moss areas, offsetting clumps of spiky oats and hops with roses and more ammobium.*

Braided straw base
(left)
A widening spray of blue and deep-pink larkspur, lavender and delicate oats falls in a semicircle, leaving part of the braid on view.

Incorporating ribbon
(below)
Pink ribbons, headed by a bow, are threaded and trailed through the vines of this wreath. Bunches of hydrangea, peach roses and gypsophila are wired in between the woody vines.

Sphagnum moss base
(below left)
A fan of grass stems, poppy seedheads and leucodendron cones partially covers the green base.

Hanging arrangements

Dried-flower ropes, hanging bunches and swags can transform a room or stairwell and are ideal when decorating the house for a special occasion. Braided ropes decorated with bunches of wired flowers and ribbon make an extremely attractive feature either side of the fireplace or along ceiling beams. A striking combination of bunches when wired together to make a globe shape and hung from the ceiling makes a truly grand centerpiece. Sturdy, chain-link swags made on a wire-and-hay base are ideal for hanging along a wall. More delicate swags made with reel wire can be hung around doors and pictures and also look lovely adorning the banisters.

Hanging spheres

A great glowing bunch, built up into a sphere of flowers and foliage, can transform a stairwell or the corner of a room. For the most striking result, choose dried materials with strong variations in texture and color and arrange them informally.

Making a hanging sphere

1 To create the stunning hanging sphere, opposite, you will need stem wires, a 1 ½ inch curtain ring, scissors, and red bottlebrush, pink helichrysum, pink and yellow roses, green amaranthus, two varieties of bupleurum, clumps of sea lavender and Leucodendron meridianum. These will be arranged boldly in clumps so that there are some larger areas of just one color. As with all arrangements, have everything ready at hand before you start.

2 Hang the curtain ring at a convenient working height. Wire separate bunches of each of the ingredients, leaving long wires for attaching. Wire the bunches to the ring one by one, leaving the stems to hang short of the ring.

3 Wire in more and more bunches, always bearing in mind where each will appear in the finished arrangement. The statice acts as the main filler while the spiky bottlebrush and the amaranthus serve to break the line of the curve.

Completed sphere
The last stage of making this spectacular orb is to make minor rearrangements of individual bunches and then to hoist it into its final position. The curtain ring at its top center will not be seen.

Hanging bunches

Both drying and dried flowers can look marvelous hanging in bunches against a wall, from a beam, or on a cupboard door. When arranging a mixed bunch of dried flowers to hang on a wall, consider carefully both the scale of the bunch and the colors you use, just as you would a painting, to ensure that it suits its location, and becomes an integral part of its surroundings. Although hanging bunches look effective alone, they also work well in combination.

Tying a mixed bunch

1 *The flowers and grasses that make up this sunny bunch are cream helichrysum, alchemilla, white larkspur,* Helichrysum italicum, *phalaris, dill and green hydrangea. Bear in mind that the finished bunch will be seen from below, so look at it head-on as you prepare it. Arrange an initial bunch, using clumps of each of the longer stems in an informal way. Tie tightly with string well below the flowerheads. You can conceal the string with ribbon when all the ties are made.*

2 *Prepare a second, denser bunch to complement the first and then tie it to the first bunch, positioning the flowerheads just a little lower.*

3 *Complete the bunch by tying in hydrangea heads at the bottom of the bunch and disguising the string ties with a bow.*

Textural bunch
It is the different textures of the flowers in this hanging bunch that make it so special. Clumps of white gypsophila accentuate groups of apricot-pink roses and spikes of Limonium suworowii. *A few stems of green amaranthus and* Limonium caspia *are balanced by the group of pink hydrangeas.*

Sunny bunch
This is the completed bunch, described in the sequence opposite – a warm and inviting addition to any room. A lemon satin bow complements the floral material and adds the finishing touch.

Flower ropes

Flower ropes can be either small, delicate affairs just a few inches long, such as a circlet for a bride, or long garlands of flowers to decorate a fireplace, table, archway or door or to entwine banisters or a balustrade. Circlets are usually made on a slender wire base (see p. 185), but for longer, more sturdy garlands chicken wire and moss bases are frequently used (see p. 183). The flower ropes illustrated here are both nearly 6 feet long so they make striking decorations on the grand scale. As both are more flexible than the chicken wire type, they would be particularly suited to spiraling down the poles of a tent for a summer wedding, or hanging either side of a wood, brick or marble fireplace.

Decorating a braided rope

1 *Complete a very thick raffia rope (see p. 185) to the length you require. Tie the ends firmly with raffia strands and trim neatly. Wire a small bunch of blue hydrangea flowers and brilliant yellow* Helichrysum italicum *(see p. 190). Attach the bunch close to the beginning of the braid by pushing the stem wire into the thickness of the braid, and bending back the end to secure. Wire similar bunches to attach later.*

2 *Prepare plumes of blue ribbon by doubling a length, wiring it as shown, and then tearing down each ribbon-end twice. Insert the wire of a ribbon plume into the braid above the flower bunch, and bend back to secure. Improve the feathery quality by pulling each section of ribbon over the back of a knife to curl it. (See the completed rope opposite.)*

Making an all-flower rope

1 *Take some red roses, pale pink larkspur and delicate bamboo,* Arundinaria nitida, *and arrange a bunch in a loose fashion to suit the wild look of the bamboo leaves. Tie the bunch together with florist's wire at the top of the bunched stems. Cover the knot with a few turns of wire, but do not cut the wire at this stage.*

2 *Holding the stems firmly, wind down their length and slip the wire through the last loop before pulling it tight in order to secure it.*

3 *Arrange a second bunch and position it lower than the first so their flowers partially overlap. Tie the second bunch to the first and knot tight. (See the completed rope right.)*

Braided rope
Flowers and ribbons are arranged in groups at intervals down the braid. Trailing ribbons were added towards the bottom of the braided rope, and a country-style raffia bow was attached at the top to cover the securing tie.

All-flower rope
The completed rope can be as long as you like, depending on how many bunches of flowers you tie on and where you intend the rope to hang. The informality of this rope makes it an ideal decoration for a country-style interior.

Swags

A swag, or festoon, of dried flowers is a flower rope designed to loop from one point to another. A series of swags is known as swagging. It is usually prepared for a special occasion, such as a party during a festive season, a wedding or a christening. Long tables covered with crisp white linen cloths and heavy with delicious food look even more wonderful with complementary swagging making soft curves along their edges. Doorways, alcoves, shelves, banister rails, fireplaces and ceiling beams, all take on a new look when decorated with these flowery festoons, whatever type you choose to make.

Making a long swag is certainly time-consuming. However, one of the great advantages of using dried flowers is that they last, and can be arranged well in advance, so there need be no last-minute panic to finish before the first guests arrive. Equally, the swags will continue to look good long after the last guests have left.

Making a swag with florist's wire

1 *One way of making a swag is to attach bunches of flowers to a wire. Flowers for this swag include hydrangea florets, roses, oats and gypsophila. First unroll sufficient florist's wire for the length of swag required. Tie a loop at this point but leave the reel attached to allow you to bind the bunch later. Wire the hydrangea florets and little bunches of gypsophila. Use them with the oats to make a nosegay, letting the oats stand a little taller. Trim any straggly stems that remain.*

2 *Place the bunch on the wire, directly on top of the loop, so that the flowers conceal it entirely. The loop will be used to fasten one end of the swag when it is completed.*

3 *Holding the bunch stems against the wire with one hand, tie the bunch firmly, using the attached spool of wire. Pass the spool under the last loop and pull tight.*

4 *Make a second bunch and hold it so that it overlaps the stems of the first bunch. Tie again with the wire and knot. Continue in this way until the swag is completed.*

Completed swags (below)
The single swag (top) looks very delicate in its pastel colors; it is, however, surprisingly strong. In contrast, the chain-link swag (bottom) has a rustic charm; trim the hay, if necessary, to maintain the shape of each link. Cover the untidy end of a swag with a ribbon.

Making a chain-link swag

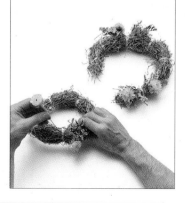

1 *Each link uses a heavy-gauge stem wire, hay, raffia ties and the selected flowers – sea lavender, helichrysum and* Limonium sinuatum. *Loop the stem wire at one end.*

2 *Tie the hay around the stem wire, with raffia strands at 3 inch intervals.*

3 *Bend the covered wire into an oval, threading the other end of the wire through the loop. Twist the wire to secure, cover with raffia and tidy the ends.*

4 *Decorate the ring with the flowers, tucking their stems under the raffia ties. Make as many individual links as necessary. Thread and join each oval through the preceding one to create the chain.*

Covering a ceiling with flowers

The inspiration for decorating a ceiling with bunches of dried flowers is the beautiful sight of cut flowers hanging to dry. If the room or corridor ceiling you have in mind has good drying conditions (see p. 198), you might indeed use freshly cut bunches that will dry and then become a permanent decoration. For drying purposes, however, freshly cut bunches must be separate from one another to allow the air to circulate between them, so you will not achieve the massed effect of the tightly packed dried bunches in the arrangement, below, while they are drying. The ceiling you use must be high enough to carry the dried flowers above head height. If it is too low, consider restricting the arrangement to a corner over a piece of furniture, such as a desk or side table. If you intend decorating an entire ceiling, you can use garden wire strung between screw-eyes to support the bunches – the wire will be hidden by the final arrangement. Where the hanging will show, consider using bamboo or brass poles, iron pipes or perhaps even iron chains from which to hang the bunches.

To decorate a whole ceiling
Secure screw-eyes in opposite walls 6 inches from the ceiling, at 10-inch intervals, and stretch strong, plastic-coated garden wire between each pair of opposing eyes. Arrange bunches of flowers and tie them 2 inches or so from the ends of the stems. The wires are gradually hidden by the hanging bunches. A great mix of colors usually works well, but the best results are achieved by arranging the bunches to vary form and texture, as well as color.

Creating large-scale wall arrangements

Placing groups of bunches or wreaths on a wall brings a special dimension to hanging dried flowers. If you have the space you can construct a complex wall hanging. The one shown below has the overlapping, massed effect of a ceiling full of hanging bunches, but flattened into two dimensions. It has the same visual interest as a rare rug or a tapestry but brings a little of the natural world indoors.

Against a white wall, the rich and varied colors and textures of dried flowers and can be displayed delightfully. If you plan to make a wall arrangement against a colored background, choose the ingredient colors carefully, bearing in mind always that they must not only combine with each other, but also suit the background color.

To make a wall frame
Mount hooks in the wall firmly, 5 feet apart, to coincide with the top edge of the flower panel. Hang a length of chain from each of these so that you can slot

6 foot bamboo poles through the links to form hanging rails. Compose your arrangement on the floor before tying the bunches to the poles on the wall. Make sure that the bunches conceal the chains.

CHAPTER SIX

FLOWERCRAFT IDEAS

Dried or preserved flower decorations do not have to be arrangements of stems in containers. All the ideas in this section exploit other ways of enjoying the beauty of flowers – and not just their appearance.

In making crystallized flowers or pot-pourri, for instance, their scent is of the same or even greater importance. The delight of slipping between cool linen sheets scented with cedar and sandalwood potpourri never seems to pall.

Equally, all of these suggestions would make wonderful gifts for friends and other loved ones. And, with a little imagination and planning, you can create a keepsake which will recall a memory you share. A nosegay or a group of pressed flowers, mounted and framed, could recapture the seasonal joys of a garden you both love, perhaps, or a summer holiday you enjoyed together. A dried-flower tree could embody some mutual flight of fantasy.

Dried flower gifts
Not only do dried flowers make special presents as arrangements, they also lend themselves to decorating and perfuming other gifts. Try making linen sachets and potpourri, or an herb pillow, scented and decorated candles, or jars and boxes of potpourri, perhaps decorated with pressed flowers. Use pressed flowers and foliage too to decorate greetings cards.

Nosegays and Bouquets

An attractive way of giving dried flowers is to make a nosegay or bouquet. A nosegay is a compact and delicate all-around bunch of flowers, while a bouquet is usually large and flat-backed. These are among the simplest arrangements of flowers to form and can be made to look formal or more natural.

When choosing plant material for a nosegay it is a good idea to use a variety of colors and textures so that the bunch can either be kept intact or split up for use in other arrangements. Dried material should be used which is bound in stem by stem. Offsetting rounded flowers with spiky material makes an attractive, eye-catching nosegay. Keeping a sense of scale in your arrangement is crucial: the most successful nosegays are compact and delicate. The flowers must not be too large and, if you are including foliage, it also should be small or with a delicate texture.

Making a nosegay

1 *Have ready a mixture of white larkspur, wired lilac-colored hydrangea florets, campanula seed-heads, quaking grass and pink statice. Begin by binding two stems together using florist's wire. Add more flowers, binding them in one by one to create a curved mound. Keep the flower-heads at differing heights for an informal country effect.*

2 *Towards completion add lower circles of flowers so that the stems are covered above the level of the wire.*

3 *Ensure that the flowers are well spaced before cutting and then tying the wire firmly. (See the completed nosegay opposite.)*

Making a simple bow

1 *Leaving a length of ribbon for one end, make a figure eight. Hold the ribbon with thumb and forefinger. Allow a generous loop of ribbon, then make a second figure eight on top of the first.*

2 *Leaving a similar length of ribbon for the other end, cut the ribbon. Pleat the center of the loops between forefinger and thumb, bind the pinched underside with wire and knot.*

3 *Using another piece of the ribbon, tie the stems of the bunch to cover any visible wiring and tie firmly. Place the bow on top of the bound stems with the ends of the binding ribbon above and below.*

4 *Tie one bow with the ends of the binding ribbon to secure it firmly in position. Check that all the ribbon ends have been cut to a similar angle and tease the completed bow into shape.*

Informal nosegay
This is the finished nosegay assembled in the step-by-step photographs opposite. It has been trimmed with a pretty, peach-pink bow that both complements the arrangement and conceals the wiring.

Dried-flower trees

A miniature "tree" made with dried flowers can look spectacular when used as a freestanding floor arrangement or, on a smaller scale placed on a low table top to look like a Bonsai tree.

First decide what height you want the tree, bearing in mind the objects which will surround it. Then, unless you are planning to create an artificial, primarily geometric shape, let nature be your guide when choosing the form the tree will take. It could be based on an oak tree or a conical-shaped bay tree, a conifer or an open-branched magnolia. Once you have decided on the shape and size of the tree you must decide on the container. The choice of container is very important and for the most successful effect you should select one large enough to create the impression that the tree might really be growing in it.

Round-headed tree and copse (opposite)
Deep red helichrysum flowers and pieces of purple Celosia argentea cristata *make the mop-headed tree on the right a particularly striking example. A foam lozenge covered in goldenrod tops several birch twigs to create the little copse on the left.*

Decorating a cone-shaped tree

1 *See page 187 for full instructions on how to make the base for this tree. Dry sphagnum moss has been pinned to cover the plastic-foam base. Push dried flower stems into the foam through the moss, using alchemilla as a background, followed by red roses, wired celosia and finally fine twigs.*

2 *Wedge the inner pot into the outer container and mound dry bun moss at the base of the trunk.*

Pressed flowers

Many flowers, grasses and leaves retain much of their color and delicacy when pressed. Narcissus, scillas, primroses and snowdrops all look very attractive; so, too, do daisy-shaped flowers and the smaller stems of heucera, forget-me-not, gypsophila and crocosmia. Fleshy plants do not usually press successfully, and full-petaled flowers, such as roses and peonies, have a tendency to look ugly because their flower-heads are too bulky and their petals overlap. However, the overlapping petals of trumpet-shaped flowers can be used to good effect to create attractive patterns.

You can make your own flower press very easily or buy one ready made. Alternatively, small pieces can be pressed between the pages of a heavy book, and larger pieces by placing them under a rug or carpet, preferably where no traffic will disturb them. Always sandwich the material between absorbent paper so that it is dried as well as pressed.

The simplest way of making your own press is to cut two pieces of plywood into rectangles about $11\frac{1}{2} \times 8$ inches. Drill holes in the corners of each piece. Insert a bolt into each hole in one piece; wing nuts will be used to clamp the wood together when the press is filled.

The most attractive way of presenting pressed flowers is to mount and frame them. Position your material on a sheet of good quality card stock – off-white or cream is usually best. Glue each piece in position, using white glue, placing a tiny spot on the centerback of it, or a clear adhesive spray. You must make sure that the material is positioned correctly first time, as it is difficult to move. Choose a simple frame that does not detract from the delicacy of the plants.

Arranging pressed material
This simple arrangement is given elegant form by pointing all the stems in the same direction. The mixture of colors and textures provides interest.

Sampler arrangement

A border of rose leaves frames groups of violas, hydrangeas, chervil and a single anemone. Rose and fern leaves make particularly effective borders, so do the silver leaves of Cineraria maritima, *and trails of small-leaved ivy can work well. Be careful not to position flowers or leaves too close to the edge of the mounting card or they may be obscured by the frame – broad margins are safest. This picture was inspired by a sampler, but botanical paintings may also stimulate ideas for your own designs. There are no hard and fast rules for designed pressed flower pictures. You could be guided by the way the plant grows, recalling the grouping of its flowers and foliage.*

Using a press

Pressing flowers with bulky centers

Place a piece of cardboard and then a folded sheet of blotting paper on the base of the press. Insert the plant material between the two "faces" of the folded blotting paper. Cover with another piece of cardboard. Continue until the press is full. The intermediate pieces of cardboard are important since they prevent plant impressions passing from layer to layer.

1 Place a piece of cardboard and then a folded sheet of blotting paper in the press. Insert the plant material into the blotting paper, arranging it on the lower of the two "faces" and then cut holes in the upper "face" to align exactly with the centers of the flowers. Close the sheet of blotting paper, covering the petals. The centers of the flowers will poke through the holes.

2 Cut a thin slice of foam to the same thickness as the centers of the flowers. Cut holes in it which will align with the flower centers and place the foam on top of the folded sheet of blotting paper. The flower centers should now be level with the top of the foam. Place a piece of cardboard carefully on top of the foam and then continue loading the press, layering the material.

Potpourri

Rose petals, lavender, mimosa, pinks, lilies, jasmine, violets and honeysuckle all retain their perfume for a long time after drying. While a mixture of such scented flowers alone will emit a delicate fragrance, a more pervasive perfume is achieved by adding herbs, spices, seeds, bark, oil and fixatives to make potpourri.

There are two methods of making potpourri: the dry and the moist. Whichever you choose, the flowers should be picked as the buds open, preferably on a dry day after any dew has evaporated.

The moist method The plant material is partly dried on sheets of absorbent material, such as blotting paper. After two days, when the petals have shrunk, all the plant material is placed in a jar in alternate layers of salt. The mixture is stirred every day for two weeks, by which time it should be crumbly. A fixative, such as orris root or tonka beans, and spices and essential oils are added and the jar sealed. The contents are then left for about six weeks to mature.

The dry method The plant material is dried completely (this takes ten days or more, depending on its density), then mixed with fixative, spices and oils, and placed in a jar to mature. The jar is sealed and shaken every day for about six weeks until ready for use.

Put potpourri in small bowls and place them around the house. To make them especially decorative, add some large, colorful dried flower petals. Potpourri will scent the air for many months, and the original perfume can be reawakened with essential oils.

Spring mix

Cottage garden mix

Lavender mix

Spicy mix

RECIPE INGREDIENTS

Spring mix (dry method)
1 cup each: lemon-scented geranium leaves, lemon verbena leaves, mimosa flowers, myrtle leaves
Grated peel of 2 lemons
¼ cup orris powder
4 drops each: citronella, rose geranium oil

Cottage garden mix (moist method)
5 cups scented pink rose petals
2 cups each: marigolds, peony petals
1 cup each: bergamot flowers, honeysuckle flowers, scented pinks
4 cups sea salt
½ cup allspice
⅓ cup orris powder
6 drops each: rose oil, rose geranium oil, bergamot oil

Lavender mix (dry method)
3 cups lavender flowers
2 cups pale pink rose leaves

1 cup each: lemon balm leaves, leptospermum leaves, sweet woodruff
Grated peel of 2 lemons
¼ cup orris powder
4 drops lavender oil

Spicy mix (moist method)
1 cup each: juniper berries, bay berries, myrtle cones, sandalwood cones, Jerusalem thorn, rose hips, bergamot flowers, rose petals
2 tbsp each: ground cinnamon, cloves
1 cup sea salt
½ cup each: sliced ginger root, pounded allspice, anise seeds, red lichen, patchouli
Grated peel of 3 oranges and 3 limes

Fragrant garden mix (moist method)
2 cups each: pale pink rose petals, Linden blossoms, white lilac flowers
1 cup each: philadelphus flowers,

lily-of-the-valley flowers, lippia leaves, chamomile flowers, white dianthus flowers, myrtle leaves, rose geranium leaves
4 cups sea salt
6 drops verbena oil
4 drops lily-of-the-valley oil
one ounce gum benzoin

Rose mix (dry method)
8 cups dried red rose petals
1 tbsp ground cloves
2 tbsp each: ground allspice, cinnamon, orris
4 drops rose oil

Woody mix (dry method)
4 cups cedar twigs
2 cups cedar bark shavings
1 cup sandalwood shavings
2 tbsp orris powder
4 drops each: cedarwood oil, sandalwood oil

Fragrant garden mix

Rose mix

Woody mix

Crystallized flowers

Crystallized flowers are easy to prepare and, as well as looking beautiful, they are delicious to eat. Almost any flowers can be crystallized, the best ones being violets, primroses and scented rose petals, while citrus blossom is a must. Because scented flowers retain much of their perfume when they are crystallized they are especially good to eat. Cherry, apple and pear blossom are all fragrant tasting, as are acacia and elderflower.

Crystallized leaves can look extremely attractive too, especially when used to make a border on top of a cake. A rich chocolate cake with fresh mint icing and filling is made all the more luscious by the addition of a border of crystallized mint leaves. Lemon balm leaves and scented geranium leaves are excellent for this purpose, too. Slices of angelica stalk (*Angelica archangelica*) are delicious when crystallized.

It is, of course, important to make quite sure that the plants you choose are not poisonous. In addition, when choosing flowers, make sure that they are of a scale to suit the dish you plan to decorate. It is a common mistake to use flowers or leaves that are too large.

Gum arabic or egg white
There are two methods of crystallizing: in one you use gum arabic to preserve the plant material and in the other you use egg white. Flowers and leaves crystallized using gum arabic last for a long time. You can buy chocolates decorated with violets or rose petals that have been crystallized in this way.

If you wish the plant material to last for many months you should use gum arabic. Dissolve ½ ounce gum arabic in ¼ cup of cold water in a double boiler or in a pot placed in a pan of simmering water. Stir until dissolved, then remove from the heat and allow the solution to cool. While it is cooling, make a syrup with ¼ cup of water and 4 ounces sugar. Boil to 176°F, then remove the pan from the heat and allow to cool.

Apply the gum arabic solution to both sides of the leaves or petals of the flowers with a paintbrush. Next, brush on the sugar solution. Finally, sift superfine sugar over the plant material, using a teaspoon to ensure that it is completely coated. Allow to dry on waxed paper.

Flowers crystallized using egg white look more beautiful than those crystallized using gum arabic, but they will not last long and should be eaten within four or five days. However, as the life of a cake or pie is fairly short, this should not present a problem. To crystallize using egg white, follow the step-by-step illustrations given opposite.

Fragrant taste of flowers (left)
This deliciously cool looking iced sponge cake is decorated with crystallized leaves and flowers, prepared using the egg-white method. The sweet-scented violets, little blue borage flowers and yellow-centered primroses are edible but the pretty, heart-shaped violet leaves are simply for decoration.

Crystallizing with egg white

1 *Beat the white of an egg lightly until it is of a frothing and even consistency. Using a paintbrush, very gently cover the petals of the flower with the beaten egg white, making sure that you give an even but light coating to both the upper and the lower surfaces. It is very important to make sure that you do not soak the petals.*

2 *Sprinkle superfine sugar carefully all over the flower, making sure that there is an even coverage. Shake off any excess sugar so the flowers are still visible through the coating. Place the flowers on a cake rack covered with waxed paper and leave in a warm place. The egg white will dry in a couple of hours.*

Crystallized flowerhead of the common camellia (Camellia japonica 'Adolphe Anderson').

CHAPTER SEVEN

DRIED FLOWERS FOR SPECIAL OCCASIONS

Life would be very dull without special occasions. The seasonal festivals – Christmas, Easter and Harvest or Thanksgiving – bring a shape and form to the year and in between there are birthdays, weddings and christenings. All of them afford us the chance to celebrate, which is what life is really about. And where there is celebration, there should be flowers.

If you are using only dried flowers for any of these occasions, they will have one great advantage over the fresh flower arrangement: you can prepare such decorations well in advance. This is invaluable if you know you will have hundreds of last-minute things to organize. The arrangements that are included in this section can all be adapted to your own particular celebrations. Let them act as a springboard for your own designs.

Birthday basket
A woody basket, fragrant with potpourri (see pp. 158–9), is filled with red roses, poppies, pink larkspur, Chinese lanterns, safflowers and Alchemilla mollis *to create a truly sumptuous present. Wrapping it in cellophane and adding red and pink satin ribbons completes what would make a wonderful gift in the depths of winter.*

Valentine's Day

The first Valentine cards date from the sixteenth century, when elaborate lace-paper cards were produced complete with verses. You could make your own Valentine card simply by writing a verse on a piece of plain card and mounting a border of pressed flowers, such as violets or primroses, on to it.

The red rose has long been a symbol of true love and is now associated with Valentine's Day. This is a more recent innovation, of course, as in colder climates roses are not in flower at this time of year and until recently were available out of season only at great expense.

However, roses dry very well, and red roses keep their intense rich color for many months if they are dried correctly. Attaching a single bloom to a present makes a poignant memento. Alternatively, an arrangement of dried flowers containing red roses, like the heart illustrated here, is a loving present.

Making a heart of red roses

1 *Make one large (1 inch) diameter moss-filled, chicken wire tube 3 feet 9 inches long and two thinner tubes, one 15 inches and the other 4 inches long (see p.183). Bend the large tube into a heart shape and join the ends at the top with wire. Using the same wire, tie on the silver-sprayed heather, overlapping each previous piece to cover the whole frame.*

2 *Take the 15-inch tube and set the 4-inch tube at right angles to one end. Tie the two together with wire to make a "T" shape, Bend the shorter tube to form the arrow-head point.*

3 *Divide the sedge into small bunches. Tie the shortest to the top of the shaft with wire and continue down two-thirds of the shaft. Tie two bunches to the head with raffia.*

Valentine heart
A heart of red roses makes a very special Valentine's Day present in true Victorian style. Silver-sprayed tree heather covers the heart-shaped base while the arrow is bound with small-headed sedge. This arrangement used 80 red roses.

4 *Place the shaft diagonally through the heart from the back until the head protrudes by 2–3 inches. Tie the shaft to the heart just under the head and near the shaft end, using wire. Attach a silver ribbon bow to the shaft to cover the last wire tie.*

5 *Decorate the heart with roses, their stems trimmed to 1 ½ inches long and a razor-sharp angle. Take care to space them evenly around the heart. Check that they are firmly in position, then cut off any protruding stems.*

Wedding Day

This day, one of the most important in many people's lives, is strongly associated with flowers. Although fresh flower bouquets look wonderful, sadly they soon wilt and die. Dried flowers, on the other hand, can be kept for many years as a keepsake. Another great advantage with dried flowers is that all the arrangements can be made in your own time, if necessary weeks in advance.

It is important to establish a color theme for the flower decorations. This does not mean that the same flowers need to be used in all the arrangements, just that the colors and general textures should match. Although an all-white wedding is beautiful, it is now more usual to mix white and cream or other pastel-colored flowers or use multi-colored mixes.

The bride's bouquet can be made to many different designs. The most important point is to make sure that the flowers are easy to hold and that the bouquet is scaled to look important but not overpowering. Nowadays, bouquets are rarely longer than 18 inches, shaped like a tear drop, and vary in style between very formal and very wild. Some brides prefer to carry a nosegay and there is also the option of carrying a beautiful bunch cradled in the arm. For bridesmaids, a nosegay is ideal.

For the wedding reception there is nothing like rich garlands and swags to add atmosphere. Used to decorate buffet tables or the poles of a tent, their handsome impact is well worth the effort involved. Arrangements can also be prepared for pedestals and table tops.

Pedestal arrangement for a reception
The flowers (many extended, see p. 189) in this soft color mix are helipterum, kangaroo paw, gypsophila, wild bamboo, Stachys lanata, and fine grass and banksia foliage. The plaster urn contains a bucket with foam piled 8 inches above its rim.

Making a spray bouquet

1 *Wire and cover every stem to be used. Make a flat-backed spray, three-quarters the length of the bouquet, binding each piece in with reel wire. Cover the wires with stem-wrap tape.*

2 *Continue to tie on pieces of plant material, fanning out the shape until they "trail" to a length that you judge is sufficient. Bend the stems as you go to form the handle which the bride will hold.*

3 *Tie on more stems to form a nosegay shape above the trail. Wired stems make arrangement very easy. Cut and tie the reel wire and trim the handle of the bouquet to 7 inches.*

4 *Make a trailing ribbon bow (see p. 153) and, using the same kind of ribbon, wind down the handle, leaving an end to tie.*

5 *Continue winding to the end of the handle and back. Knot the ribbon ends and use the ends to tie on the bow.*

Casual elegance (right)
When complete, the spray bouquet is a formal arrangement, although its outline is deliberately irregular.

Ready for the celebrations (right)
*Swags of flowers have been tacked to the edge of the
wedding-cake table, with glossy trailing bows added
to cover the ends. The cake is encircled with a single
row of helichrysum and rose heads, and a small
arrangement decorates the top. Beside the cake is the
bride's bouquet and on the chair, in front of the
pedestal, are the bride's head-dress and bridesmaid's
nosegay. It can be carried by a bridesmaid of any
age. For a very young girl, a little basket of flowers
would be a perfect solution, as it is small, light
and easy to hold. A pretty little
sphere of flowers would be
a popular choice for 5–10-
year-olds.*

Bridal bouquet (above)
*This simple bunch arrangement is made with flowers
which match the other floral decorations, including
bright pink roses, gypsophila, pale creamy pink
helichrysum, yellow kangaroo paw, oats and some
feathery foliage. Use the longest stems first and make
absolutely sure that all the thorns are removed from
the rose stems before you begin.*

Harvest time and Thanksgiving

Autumn comes and with it sadness at the loss of the long and easy summer days, but also a sense of something gained. As the crops are gathered in, as the evenings become colder, it is the time to give thanks for all that nature supplies – an ideal time for a party.

It is also an ideal time for dried flowers. The bunches that were gathered in summer and early autumn are dry and ready to be used, and the autumn spectrum of colors – glowing golds, rusts and oranges – are a joy to arrange. Think of the warmth of brightly colored flowers like deep red pom-pom dahlias, goldenrod, brilliant orange Chinese lanterns and the many colors of hydrangeas. Consider too the ripened field grains, wild grasses and seedheads.

Stores and markets at this time are full of fruits and vegetables with the same glowing colors – red apples, golden pears, gourds – and there is no reason why you should not mix these with dried flowers both in arrangements and in swags and garlands. Use nature's wealth to welcome your friends with a display which celebrates the year's harvest.

Welcoming hallway (below)
The swagging around the doorway frames a matching wreath on the door based on a circle of twisted vines (see p.184). A splendid barley sheaf stands to the left of the door. On the right a two-tier table is decorated above with a golden turban squash, a mug filled with dried barley, grasses and Chinese lanterns and a hay-covered cornucopia (see p.181), and below with several smaller arrangements.

Making the harvest swag

1 *Use a hay-filled roll of chicken wire for the swag base (see p. 183); it may be necessary to join several to achieve the required length. Wire bunches of Chinese lanterns, barley and hay (see p. 190). Wire fresh apples through their cores, bend over the end of the emerging wire and then pull it back into the core.*

2 *Push heavy-gauge stem wire into each ear of corn and wind it around the stem to secure. Cover all wires with stem-wrap tape (see p. 178). Arrange bunches of plant material along the swag, each overlapping the last, and twist the wires into the base. Wire in corn and apples at intervals.*

Making a sheaf

Take a generous bunch of black-eared barley and, using three-quarters of it, make a central core of stems, building up gradually, adding layer on layer and winding each layer with string. Use the final quarter of stems to form an outer layer, securing it to the inner core with a single knot positioned high up the stems so that they splay sideways in a spiral. Trim the stalk ends carefully and the central column will act as a pedestal. Add a braided raffia circlet to cover the binding (see p.185). Seeding grasses, rushes, grains and reeds should be picked at their prime. They are all easy to dry and can be either laid flat on paper or left standing in vases without water.

Christmas

Christmas, or Christ's Mass, has been celebrated as the birth of Christ on 25 December since the early part of the fourth century AD. Before that the Emperor Aurelian chose 25 December as the birthday of the unconquered sun and, to this day, Christmas contains elements of the winter rites linked with the solar calendar called the Kalends.

When we decorate houses with greenery and colored lights and exchange presents we are performing part of the ancient pagan rites. In fact, that most pagan of all plants, mistletoe, was allowed into the home and the Church only after Pope Gregory I agreed that pagan customs should be assimilated into Christianity.

Dried flowers can be used in Christmas decorations to stunning effect either on their own or mixed with fresh greenery such as pine, yew and holly. Many varieties of conifer such as blue pine, Scots pine and Irish yew, dry well.

If you use dried flowers mixed with the foliage from one or more conifers, you have the advantage that you can make your Advent wreaths, basket arrangements, garlands and even trees well in advance of Christmas in the knowledge that they will last throughout the whole of the festive season. But if you wish to make some garlanding using dried material and the bright red berries and rich green foliage of holly, add the holly just before Christmas as both its leaves and berries will soon wilt in a warm room.

Christmas color

Brightly colored dried flowers, such as Chinese lantern, red helichrysum, red roses and bottlebrush, look dashing against the dark rich greens of Christmas trees and foliage. So, too, do the ice-cool whites, silvers and pale blues of gypsophila and larkspur, helichrysum, senecio and santolina foliage, and hydrangea and pale blue larkspur. Anything goes when you are decorating a tree and a great mixture of

flowers and colors always looks wonderful. However, a tree decorated in one or two colors, perhaps red and green, pink and silver or orange and gold, can look as stunning as one bedecked with every color under the sun.

Ropes of dried flowers and foliage will brighten the house during the Christmas season. Fireplaces, doorways and staircases, tables, shelves and pictures are given new life when surrounded by garlanding (see pp. 146–7 for techniques). Using rich green foliage provides an added brilliance, but ropes made entirely from dried material can also be stunning and dried-flower ropes too can be made at your leisure, well before Christmas.

Cool, elegant tree (above and opposite)
Silver-sprayed baskets filled with dried hydrangea heads (see the detail above) and crisp, white, dried gypsophila dusted with glitter adorn this unusual and charming tree. Other tree decorations from dried flowers can be equally effective. Stick together groups of four or five brightly colored helichrysum heads to form small spheres and hang them beside the more traditional glass and paper decorations. Little nosegays of multicolored flowers also look very attractive.

Dramatic swagging (above)
The asymmetric swagging over the hearth dominates this interior. Two swags were made, each by overlapping a series of bunches (see p. 146). The plant material includes dried pine branches, helichrysum, twigs with silver-glittered cones, leptospermum and fresh, variegated holly. The flower-pot arrangement on the hearth is a chicken wire sphere (see p. 186) covered with dyed-green lichen and dotted with bright red berries on wires.

Festive spray
(above)
*Three branches of blue
spruce, each 2 feet
long, and some silver-
coned twigs form the
basis of this spray
decked with helichrysum
clusters and pink satin
balls. Ribbons cascade
from a bow covering
the tie.*

**Tea caddy
arrangement**
(above right)
*Twigs and eucalyptus
leaves were sprayed with
silver paint and glitter
dust for a festive look.*

Formal centerpiece
(right)
*A massed chicken wire
base (see p.183) is
decorated with clematis
seedheads, roses,
helichrysum, green
hydrangeas, lichen
and agonis and
osmunda fern.*

CHAPTER EIGHT

TOOLS, MATERIALS AND TECHNIQUES

The tools and materials required for making fresh- and dried-flower arrangements are few and simple. All you need is shown in this section, together with the necessary, though straight-forward, techniques you should master to be sure of a professional finish to your work, whether in containers or on bases. Become proficient at these techniques and you will be able to tackle all the arrangements shown in this book and feel confident of making up your own creations for all sorts of occasions.

The following pages also contain the practical details of air drying fresh flowers, drying with desiccants, preserving with glycerine and coloring plant material, as well as how to store plant material once it has been dried.

An ideal workspace
Few of us can enjoy the luxury of a room set aside for conditioning, arranging, drying and storing flowers and foliage, but with imagination it is possible to make use of smaller spaces. For instance, a prettily painted hanging cupboard placed in a hall or stairway could easily be fitted out for storing dried flowers and other plant materials. Make sure the cupboard has good air circulation.

Tools and materials

There is a very wide range of equipment available to the professional flower arranger, but many items are useful only on the odd occasion. Set out below are the materials and tools used for the arrangements in this book. The essential items are high-quality florists' scissors, a sharp steel knife and some foam. The others are regularly useful and can be purchased at many florists or craft stores.

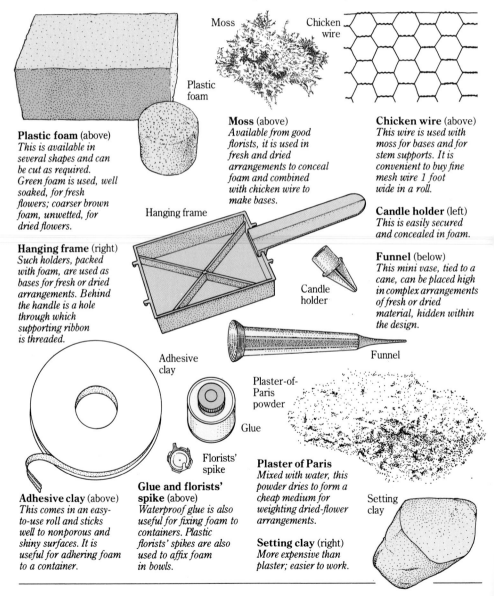

Plastic foam (above)
This is available in several shapes and can be cut as required. Green foam is used, well soaked, for fresh flowers; coarser brown foam, unwetted, for dried flowers.

Hanging frame (right)
Such holders, packed with foam, are used as bases for fresh or dried arrangements. Behind the handle is a hole through which supporting ribbon is threaded.

Moss

Chicken wire

Plastic foam

Hanging frame

Moss (above)
Available from good florists, it is used in fresh and dried arrangements to conceal foam and combined with chicken wire to make bases.

Chicken wire (above)
This wire is used with moss for bases and for stem supports. It is convenient to buy fine mesh wire 1 foot wide in a roll.

Candle holder (left)
This is easily secured and concealed in foam.

Funnel (below)
This mini vase, tied to a cane, can be placed high in complex arrangements of fresh or dried material, hidden within the design.

Candle holder

Funnel

Adhesive clay

Plaster-of-Paris powder

Glue

Florists' spike

Setting clay

Adhesive clay (above)
This comes in an easy-to-use roll and sticks well to nonporous and shiny surfaces. It is useful for adhering foam to a container.

Glue and florists' spike (above)
Waterproof glue is also useful for fixing foam to containers. Plastic florists' spikes are also used to affix foam in bowls.

Plaster of Paris
Mixed with water, this powder dries to form a cheap medium for weighting dried-flower arrangements.

Setting clay (right)
More expensive than plaster; easier to work.

Florists' scissors

Knives

Wire cutters

Pruning shears

Medium-gauge
15½ inch
stem wire

Fine-gauge
11 inch
stem wire

Fine-gauge
9 inch
stem wire

Fine-gauge
6 inch
stem wire

6 inch
rose wire

Cutting tools
*Florists' scissors are
used for cutting most
plant material and thin
wires. You also need a
steel knife for scraping
stems and a long-bladed
knife for cutting foam,
pruning shears for
cutting heavy stems and
wire cutters for cutting
heavy-gauge wires and
chicken wire.*

**Stem-wrap tape
and florists' tape**
*Stem-wrap tape is
rubber-based and used
for binding wired stems
of fresh or dried material
to give a natural
appearance. It is
available in green,
brown and white.
Florists' tape is a crêpey,
lighter material which
some people find easier
to use. It is available
in several colors.*

String

Spool wire

Rose wire

Stem-wrap tape

Florists' tape

Raffia

**String, spool wire and
rose wire** (below)
*Used for binding wired
stems. Rose wire is
silver and comes in two
gauges. Spool wire is
thicker and black.
String must be strong
but not too thick.*

Raffia (below)
*Its natural color makes
it a good base for braided
wreaths and garlands.*

Straight wires
*Stem wires (for false
stems) range from
3½ to 18 inches in length
and from heavy to fine
gauge. Fine silver rose
wires, for more delicate
work, are 6 inch
long. Cane is an
alternative for heavy-
headed stems.*

Preparing containers

Although it is not necessary to prepare every single container for displaying flowers – natural-looking arrangements are often best displayed simply in a pitcher – flower arranging is often much simpler if the stems are held in supporting material.

Foam (see p. 178) is the most efficient supporting material. It is easy to sculpt and, if your container is especially large, you can always put two pieces together and secure both on the bottom on florists' spikes (see p. 178). If you are preparing a fresh-flower arrangement, make sure that the foam is thoroughly soaked before you use it and fill the container with water once the arrangement is complete. If your container

has incurving sides, chicken wire might be a good alternative, and, for a simple arrangement in a glass container, marbles or pebbles will hold stems in position.

If you are preparing a glass container with wet foam and you wish to conceal it, simply surround it with moss: it loves the water. The stems of dried material are generally unattractive and look particularly ugly seen through the sides of a glass vase. This problem is easily overcome by lining the inside of the container – between glass and foam – with potpourri or moss.

Some containers will require lining before you fill them with water! Others will need to be adapted or decorated.

Preparing a ceramic container

Far left: For a bowl which curves outward, secure foam sculpted to fit to a florists' spike affixed to the bottom of the bowl with adhesive clay. To prepare a shallow, saucer-shaped container, stick a sculpted mound of foam to the base with glue (a waterproof type if preparing a fresh arrangement).

Left: As an alternative to a foam support for a container which curves inwards, you can stretch a piece of chicken wire inside the rim and pull it upward until it grips the lipped sides.

Lining a porous container for fresh flowers

1 *Place a plastic bowl of appropriate size inside the container. You may need to pack the space between basket and container with foam. Affix a florists' spike to the bottom of the bowl with adhesive clay.*

2 *Using a sharp knife, sculpt a piece of wet foam to fit the bowl and affix it securely to the florists' spike on the base of the bowl.*

3 *Insert damp moss to conceal, packing between the sides of the container and bowl, if necessary, and also on top of the wet foam.*

Preparing a glass container

1 *Affix two florists' spikes to the bottom of the container with adhesive clay. Sculpt a block of foam, wet if arranging fresh flowers, to fit neatly inside the container.*

2 *Secure the foam on the florist's spikes in the center of the container. Surround and cover the foam with clumps of damp moss. If using taller cylinder shapes for dried-flower arrangements, pressed autumnal leaves placed between glass and moss look good.*

Decorating a container with paper

Glue scraps of colorful paper to the inside of the clear container, overlapping each piece with the next to create a "mosaic" effect. Varnish to prevent the paper from peeling. Place a lining vase inside the decorated container.

Adapting a wastepaper basket

1 *Place two strands of raffia on the floor, and cover with a thick layer of hay. Roll the wastepaper basket carefully over the hay, using the raffia to hold it in place around the sides of the container.*

2 *Tie the ends of the raffia into bows, and add further ties if necessary to secure the hay in place. Trim untidy sections with scissors. (See the wicker horn-shape covered in this way on p. 171.)*

Preparing bases

Achieving a professional and satisfying result when arranging flowers involves good groundwork. Time spent preparing saves arranging time later on. This includes time spent making your own wreath, sphere and tree bases if you want an alternative to store bought varieties.

Store-bought bases are usually made from plastic foam, but wire frames of various types are commercially available and these you can cover with moss. It is even more satisfying to make your own frame, using one of the methods shown, as you have full control of its design.

We know from paintings and sculptures that wreaths (rigid circles of flowers and/or foliage) have been traditional wall or door decorations since early times, especially wreaths of sweet-smelling flowers and aromatic herbs. There are several different methods of making bases for circular arrangements. You can weave supple stems together to form a frame or roll chicken wire around sphagnum moss to form a long sausage and sew the ends together to make a circle. Chicken wire is very useful for flower arrangers: it can also be used (with foam) for the base of a dried-flower sphere or for thick garlands and swags of fresh or dried plant material. For a delicate circlet of dried flowers stem wire (see p. 179) is all you need to make a base.

Making bases for wreaths, spheres and ornamental trees entails using damp or sticky plant material which must be left to dry thoroughly before it is used with dried flowers or your arrangement will quickly spoil. Drying can take up to a week.

Making a simple moss base

1 *Choose a commercially available wire frame and attach the end of a reel of string to it, leaving a short length beyond the knot. Take a generous clump of damp moss.*

2 *Holding the moss against the frame, tie it on securely with string. Continue winding around the frame, overlapping the clumps.*

3 *Overlap the last clump of moss with the first and tie it on. Cut the string and tie the end to the original knot end to make a neat finish. Let the moss dry thoroughly before using dried flowers.*

Making a circular moss and chicken-wire base

1 *Cut a piece of 1 foot chicken wire to the length of the circumference you want. Lay it flat, and arrange damp sphagnum moss along one edge. Roll the wire tightly over the moss to form a solid tube approximately 3 inches thick. Tuck in the moss and turn in any sharp wires as you roll.*

2 *Bend the tube around evenly to form a circle, gradually curving it to keep the circle smooth. Do not overlap the ends; these will be sewn together neatly.*

3 *Attach spool wire to one end of the chicken-wire tube, leaving a loose end for finishing. Sew the two ends of the tube together, and knot and conceal the wire ends. Sphagnum moss is commercially available, from any good florist or store. Remember to let it dry out thoroughly before use if making a dried-flower arrangement.*

Making a vine wreath

1 *The stems of various climbing plants and certain particularly supple tree branches can be used to make wreath bases. The wood must be supple and cut into pieces roughly 4 ½ feet long. The stems of the vine* Actinidia chinensis *and branches of willow and birch make particularly handsome bases. Make a circle of the required size with one stem of your chosen material and secure it firmly.*

2 *Take another stem, engage it near the binding, and then twine it carefully around the first ring and secure the end firmly.*

3 *Continue to wind in the pieces of vine, allowing oddly shaped stems to create holes, until you reach the thickness you require. Cut away the wire once the circle is self-supporting. If the base is to be used for a dried-flower arrangement, let it dry out completely before attaching any flowers. A wreath need not be packed with material around its entire circumference. A vine wreath is decorative, and you can allow it to show through, or leave a portion bare for a dynamic effect.*

Making a delicate circlet

1 *Make small bunches of ingredients. Join two stem wires, twisting an "eye" in one end and trimming the other to 2 inches longer than the circumference of the head. Cover with stem-wrap tape.*

2 *Tie on the bunches using spool wire, covering each binding with tape. Hide the "eye" with the first bunch and the stems of each bunch with the flowers of the next. Leave 1 inch of wire free.*

3 *Bend the decorated wire into a circle. Thread the free wire through the "eye" and bend it back to secure. The flowers of the first bunch on the stem wire should cover the stems of the last bunch.*

Making a braided loop

1 *Attach a good bunch of raffia strands, as thick as the required base, to a firm support. Divide the raffia into three equal portions and weave the left portion and then the right portion alternately over the central portion until you reach the end of the strands. Tie the ends firmly with raffia and trim.*

2 *A raffia braid can be sewn to form a circular base for a dried-flower wreath as below, or used as a base for a garland or swag.*

Making a moss-covered ball

Moss-covered balls are most commonly used for hanging arrangements, but they can provide the base *for a round-headed, dried-flower tree (see opposite) or for a little bridesmaid's ball of dried flowers which can be simply carried on a looped ribbon.*

1 *Cut a length of 1 foot wide chicken wire, a little longer than the planned circumference of the ball. Make a mound of foam pieces on the wire; the foam will be dry if you are making a dried-flower arrangement, and wet if you are arranging fresh flowers. Hold the foam pieces in place with one hand and lift an edge of the wire with the other.*

2 *Holding the first wire edge firmly in place, lift and fold in the remaining edges gently, adding or subtracting pieces of foam to fill out the sphere shape as becomes necessary. Then mold the chicken wire and foam to improve the shape, removing uneven or flat areas where appropriate, and turn sharp wire ends inward.*

3 *Knot the end of a spool of wire (see p. 179) to the mesh, leaving an end long enough for finishing. Apply patches of moss (dry for dried-flower arrangements, damp for fresh) and hold them in place, winding the wire around the outside to secure them. If you use dark-colored wire, it will not show against the moss, so use plenty.*

4 *When you begin your arrangement, you will be pushing stems and wires through the moss into the foam so it is important to make the covering very firm. Once the whole ball is covered with moss, bring the wire back to the long end of the starting knot and tie together. Trim the ends and conceal them within the moss.*

Making a tree base
Cone-shaped and round-headed trees are popular geometrical designs, but you may prefer to make *nature your guide when selecting a shape. The trunk must be firm and the base weighty, so the trunk is set in plaster of Paris in an inner pot.*

1 *Line a small clay pot with slivers of dry foam. Plaster of Paris expands as it sets, and the pieces of foam will allow room for expansion and prevent the pot from cracking. Mix plaster of Paris powder to a thick, creamy consistency with water. Fill the pot two-thirds full with the mixture, making sure that the foam slivers stay in place.*

2 *Place the trunk quickly in the plaster – you will feel it reach the base. Wobble it to ensure that the plaster adheres all around. Supporting the trunk with one hand, turn the pot slowly to see that it looks right from every angle, and then spoon in more plaster to fill the pot to within ½ inch of the rim. Support the trunk until it stands by itself.*

3 *Keep some water handy to pour into the plaster of Paris mixing bowl as soon as you have scooped out as much as you need. This will prevent it from setting and cracking the bowl. You can now begin making the head of the tree. Press your chosen foam base-shape firmly onto the trunk. Foam cones and spheres are obtainable from florists but you can sculpt your own from a plastic foam "brick". The moss-covered ball described on p.186 would serve as a base for a round-headed tree. Make staples by bending short, fine-gauge stem wires double, and use them to pin dry sphagnum moss to the cone.*

Hanging loops

All hanging flower arrangements (such as wreaths, hanging bunches, balls and swags) need to have a loop of some sort attached to them so that they can be held in position. The loop you choose should complement your work so that, even from the back, the design is pleasing to the eye. There is only one golden rule: use materials strong enough to support the hanging arrangement over a long period. These examples use raffia and wire. The braided raffia technique is stronger than the sewn method; the wire loop, securely fixed, is even stronger.

Making a raffia loop

Following the instructions on p.185, make a raffia braid to the required thickness and length. Form a loop with the braid and tie the cross-over tightly using a stem wire, leaving ends that can be attached to a base. To make a lightweight loop, take several strands of raffia, and enclose them in the looped end of a stem wire before twisting the "eye" shut. Using the wire like a needle, push it through the base. Repeat in the opposite direction to form a loop. Cut the wire free and knot the raffia.

Making a wire loop

1 *Cover a wire with stem-wrap tape (see p.179), twist a circle in its middle, and push both ends into the back of the base.*

2 *Pull the two ends back under the base and then push each end into the moss, one on either side of the loop, to secure.*

3 *The wire loop appears in the middle of the back of the base with its wire ends tucked in neatly and securely.*

Wiring plant material

Wiring fresh plant material is usually only necessary when an arrangement requires the flowers and foliage to be contorted into very precise positions, as with wedding nosegays, rings, pew ends and complicated garlands. In contrast, dried flowers and foliage often need to be wired to compensate for either the shortness or the fragility of their stems.

Choose a suitable stem wire (see p. 179) – one that will give adequate flexibility and strength as well as the length of stem required. Stem-wrap tape (see p. 179) is used to disguise the unsightly wire.

Lengthening or strengthening stems

1 Cut the flower leaving 1 inch of stem. Place a stem wire against the stem and a fine rose wire against this so that the longer portion of rose wire protrudes upwards.

2 Bend the longer end down and begin to spiral it tightly around the stem, lower end of the rose wire and stem wire.

3 Continue winding the rose wire downward for 3 inches to hold the stem firmly in place. Cut the rose wire and fold the end in neatly.

> **SUITABLE PLANTS**
> *Flowers with thin stems, such as fresh freesia*

Wiring lily-of-the-valley

1 Make a ⅛ inch U-shape with the end of a fine rose wire. Hook it near the top of the flower stem, so that the remainder of the wire runs down parallel to the spire of flowers.

2 Very gently begin twisting the rose wire around the stem between each single flower, being careful not to break the stem. Continue winding the rose wire down the stem until it is below the lowest flower.

3 Wire the remainder of the stem as shown in the previous method.

> **OTHER SUITABLE PLANTS**
> *Small trails of fresh ivy leaves*

Wiring flowerheads: method 1

Choose a stem wire of the right gauge to support the flowerhead firmly. Cut the flower, leaving 1 ½ inches of stem. Push the wire up the stem and into the base of the flower.

SUITABLE PLANTS
Rose, carnation, spray carnation, small lily, orchid

Wiring flowerheads: method 2

Proceed as for method 1. Push the wire through the flowerhead. Bend the wire into a small U shape and pull it downwards, drawing the U-shaped end through the flower. Squeeze the wire ends together.

SUITABLE PLANTS
Single chrysanthemum or rose, helichrysum

Wiring hollow or broken stems

Carefully insert a piece of stem wire of appropriate length and gauge to fit inside the entire stem. Hollow stems can be extended or mended using similar methods; cover the work with stem-wrap tape.

SUITABLE PLANTS
Delphinium, hyacinth, larkspur, ranunculus

Wiring bunches

Holding the bunch in one hand, place a medium-gauge stem wire on top of the stems, its lower end level with their ends. Use the thumb to secure it. Taking the free end of the wire in the other hand, bend it behind the stems at a point 2 inches up from the stem ends. Continue winding it down around the short end and the stems. Use the remaining wire to form an extension of the stems, if required.

Wiring cones

1 *Use heavy-gauge stem wire to form a stem for a cone. Push one end of the wire horizontally through the lowest band of scales so 2 inches juts out on the other side. Wind that end of the wire tightly back around the cone. Twist the wire ends together so that the cone is held firmly.*

2 *Bend the twisted ends under the cone so that the long wire forms a stem from the center of the base of the cone. Trim the shorter end neatly and conceal the whole length of the wire with stem-wrap tape as described below.*

Concealing wired stems

1 *Holding the wired flowerhead upside down, place a piece of stem-wrap tape behind the stem and at an angle of 45°.*

2 *Holding the stem-wrap tape so that it is stretched taut, revolve the wired stem so that the tape covers itself in a spiral up the wire. Twist to seal the tape at the lower end of the wire.*

Conditioning fresh plant material

Having prepared the container or base and collected the plant material, it is well worth pausing to prepare the material before you make your arrangement. With a little attention at this stage the flowers will last longer and look more attractive.

Even if you have only just cut the stems from the plant, you should always cut them anew at a sharp, diagonal angle to expose a wider surface area. Next, strip all the lower leaves from the stems, otherwise they will simply rot in the water. Remove thorns too. Milky stems should be singed to prevent them from oozing in the vase. And the uppermost buds (which will never flower) of particularly tall plants should be removed. Scraping the bottom of the sturdier green stems and slitting *and* scraping the bottom of woody stems helps them to take up water.

Some plant material seems to benefit enormously from the so-called "boiling-water treatment". Although it may seem a drastic measure, the technique forces air down and out of the stems as the hot water rises upwards, so eliminating airlocks which prevent water from reaching flower-heads and the tips of foliage. Without this treatment, some young plant material can wilt badly, and it can also solve the problem of drooping rose heads.

Finally, stand all plant material in deep water a few hours before arranging, pouring water into hollow stems first.

Preparing stems for arrangement

1 Scraping
With a sharp knife or florist's scissors, scrape the bark from the last 2 inches of the stem to encourage it to take up water more quickly and efficiently.

2 Slitting
With a pair of florists' scissors, very carefully cut upward from the base of the stem, making a cut approximately 2 inches long.

3 Recutting
With florists' scissors, cut the slit stem diagonally to expose a greater surface area to the water.

SUITABLE PLANTS
For scraping, slitting and recutting: robust stems such as azalea, camellia, ceanothus, eucalyptus. For slitting and recutting: most green stems

---

Filling hollow stems: method 1

1 *To ensure that water reaches the flowerhead quickly, making it last longer, hold the stem upside down and carefully pour in water.*

2 *When the stem is full, plug the end with a small piece of wet cotton wool and place the stem in a vase of water immediately.*

Filling hollow stems: method 2

1 *Pour water into the stem as above, and then place your thumb tightly over the end.*

2 *Upend the stem into a vase filled with water, preferably the one you will be using, keeping your thumb over the end until it is immersed.*

SUITABLE PLANTS FOR EITHER METHOD
Amaryllis, Queen Anne's lace, delphinium, hippeastrum, larkspur, lupine.

Removing top buds

Singeing milky stems

To allow the buds lower down a long stem to drink some water and therefore increase their chances of eventually flowering, remove the topmost buds (which are extremely unlikely ever to flower) with a pair of florists' scissors. If you take time and care it is not that difficult to *trim in such a way that the cut will not be seen by any but the very closest observer.*

SUITABLE PLANTS
Gladiolus, kaffir lily, tuberose

To seal an oozing stem, singe the cut end with a lighted match. This will prevent unsightly discoloration of the water and extend the life of the material.

SUITABLE PLANTS
Euphorbia, fern, poppy

Boiling-water treatment

1 *Pour about 2 inches of water into a pan and bring the water to the boil. While waiting for the water to boil, half fill a bucket with tepid water. Having removed the pan to a sturdy table, hold the plant material diagonally and place the ends of the stems in the boiling water for 20 seconds. The stems are held diagonally to prevent the steam affecting the flowers and leaves. Protect short-stemmed flowers with a plastic bag secured with a rubber band.*

2 *Remove the material from the boiling water and immediately plunge the stems into the bucket of tepid water. Let them stand in this deep water for several hours before beginning your arrangement so that flowers and foliage can take a good, long drink.*

SUITABLE PLANTS
Angelica, bamboo, bear's breeches, black-eyed Susan butterfly bush, cock'scomb, chervil, dogwood, gerbera, globe flower, hollyhock, knotweed, laburnum, magnolia, mallow, monkshood, Queen Anne's lace, sunflower, wormwood.

Reviving foliage
Most foliage and some flowers can be refreshed or revived before beginning your arrangement either by totally submerging them in a suitably-sized container filled with cool water or by running cool water over them for five minutes. In some instances, when dealing with particularly large pieces of foliage for large-scale arrangements, a bath may be the only available option.

Straightening stems

1 *To make flexible stemmed flowers easier to arrange, cut them on the diagonal, and then wrap them in newspaper in bunches of four or five.*

2 *Secure each newspaper bunch with adhesive tape and place in a bucket of water. Leave overnight in a cool place and then use in an arrangement.*

SUITABLE PLANTS
Euphorbia, gerbera, poppy, rose, tulip

Looking after arrangements

Cut flowers do not need a lot of care if they have been prepared appropriately. However, there are some basic guidelines that will ensure that your arrangements last longer. For instance, it is important not to place fresh flowers directly in front of a radiator, or in strong direct sunlight, as the heat will cause the flowers to droop remarkably quickly. Adding a few drops of bleach and a teaspoon of sugar to the water in the container will prolong the life of the plant material, and changing the water regularly helps to keep it fresh-smelling. Removing flowerheads as they die keeps the arrangements looking attractive for a longer period of time.

Air drying plant material

Air drying is the easiest and most effective method of preserving plant material and most of the plants used in the dried-flower arrangements in this book have been air dried. Depending on the type of plant, the material can be dried hanging upside down, standing upright in a container, or simply lying on the floor.

Ideally, plant material should be air dried in a room that is cool, dry, well-ventilated and dark, although you can air dry flowers in warmer temperatures and in a room or cupboard without a moving air current. However, it is imperative that the drying room is both dry and dark. If it is not dry, the plant material will rot, especially where the stems or flowers are touching, such as at the tying point of a hanging bunch. If the room is not dark, the flowers will fade extremely quickly.

Harvesting for air drying

All plant material should be picked in dry weather, preferably around or after midday, when any dew will have evaporated. Flowers should be picked approximately four days before they reach their prime. In other words, for the best possible effect a rose should always be picked when the bud is colorful and just as it is on the very point of opening.

Hang drying

Hanging material to dry is the most common method of air drying. Remove all the lower leaves, wipe away any moisture on the stems and then tie the stems together into bunches with lengths of raffia or string, or even a rubber band. Make sure the stems beneath the tie are short enough to be able to hang the bunches upside down in position. Fan out the flowers, seedheads and leaves in each bunch so that there is as little contact between the leaves and petals as possible. Then attach the bunches or single stems upside down to a beam, wire or length of string in your drying place.

Drying upright or flat

Some material air dries well when placed upright in a container, either standing in a small amount of water that slowly evaporates, or simply in an empty vase. As with hanging bunches, the material needs to stand in a cool, dry, well-ventilated, dark place for best results.

Most deciduous and many evergreen leaves are better dried flat, although the leaves will develop crinkly edges. Moss and fir cones can be laid in an airy box or basket to dry and you can sit larger heads of plants such as artichokes on a chicken wire shelf.

Bunching fresh-cut stems

Remove the lower leaves and any thorns to leave bare stems. Assemble a bunch of about five flowers, staggering the positions of the flowerheads. Tie the stems loosely together with string or raffia. Spread out the flowers so that the heads and leaves are well separated and the air can circulate freely around them as they dry.

Spraying grasses and rushes

The seedheads of some grasses, especially pampas grass and bulrushes, break up during drying if their surface is not sealed. Spray liberally (out of doors, if possible) with ozone-friendly hair spray or another fixative to prevent them from disintegrating.

Hanging to dry

Hanging bunches of plant stems upside down to dry is one of the simplest methods of air drying. Set up a series of poles or wires about 10 inches apart and at least 8 inches below the ceiling to ensure good air circulation. Either hook the bunches over the poles or attach them to the support with string or raffia ties.

Bunching wired stems

Flowers wired when fresh are very easy to hang dry. Bunch about ten flowerheads together and bind with a rubber band. Gently bend the stem wires so that none of the flowerheads touch. Hang upside-down to dry.

Drying on a pole
This is the quickest way to air dry climbers such as hops and clematis which have attractive seedheads. Cut them while they are still fresh and wind them around a suspended bamboo pole.

Drying heavy-headed flowers
Secure chicken wire horizontally and high enough to allow long stems to hang freely. Slot each stem through the mesh. Leave the husks of decorative corn in place during drying.

SUITABLE PLANTS
Carline thistle, globe artichoke, lotus, onion, protea, decorative corn.

Cones
Leave cones at room temperature for a few days until no moisture is apparent between the scales.

Moss and lichen
Lay in a single layer on a bed of crumpled newspaper. Do not pack tightly.

Drying upright in a container

There are two methods of air drying plant material upright. Some plants dry well when left standing in an empty vase (left). Others dry better when stood in about 2 inches of water. The stems will absorb some of the water, which gradually evaporates, leaving the plant material to dry out completely.

SUITABLE PLANTS
With water: gypsophila, hybrid delphinium, hydrangea, lachenalia, mimosa
Without water: bulrush, chenopodium, onion, pampas, sea lavender

Drying flat

Lay the material on an absorbent surface: cardboard or newspaper is ideal. Space the plant material out carefully so that air can circulate around the stems and leaves. Leaves shrivel when dried in this way but keep their color and retain their natural shape on the stem, which is not the case if they are dried upright or hanging.

SUITABLE PLANTS
Bamboo, all grasses, lavender

Using desiccants

Most plant material can be dried effectively using desiccants, or drying agents, such as silica gel, borax, alum or fine sand. Desiccants draw the moisture out of plant material while leaving it otherwise relatively unchanged, so material dried by this method most closely resembles its fresh original in color, size and texture. However, there are some drawbacks to using desiccants. Silica gel, which dries material the quickest, is very expensive (although crystals can be dried in the oven and reused), and all desiccants are tricky to place around the material that you are drying. Also, since they tend to make plant material rather brittle, it is a good idea to wire flowerheads and leaves before drying them (see p. 189).

Silica gel
Silica gel is available as white crystals, or as color-indicator crystals, which are blue when dry but turn pink as they absorb moisture. Some must be ground down in a pestle and mortar or coffee grinder (wash thoroughly afterwards) to a smaller size to envelop material efficiently.

You will need an airtight tin or box large enough to hold the material you wish to dry. Place a layer of dry crystals in the container and lay the material on top. Pile the crystals around it, using a fine brush to make sure that every part is surrounded by desiccant. Place the lid on the container and seal it with tape. Check the material after two days: it should be firm, and the crystals should be pink. Remove the material from the container as soon as it is dry, otherwise it will become brittle.

Borax, alum and silver sand
Borax and alum should be mixed with fine dry sand before use as desiccants: three parts chemical to two parts sand. Material placed in either will take about ten days to dry; plant material dried in sand alone will take about three weeks.

SUITABLE PLANTS
Anemone, camellia, dahlia (small varieties), delphinium, freesia, gentian, gerbera, hellebore, larkspur, lily, narcissus, peony, ranunculus, rose, zinnia.

Using silica gel

1 *A cookie tin is an ideal container for drying using silica gel. Cover the base of the tin with crystals, and place plant material on top. Remember that heavy stems do not survive this method so replace with wire (see p. 190) before using desiccant.*

2 *Spoon the crystals around the material and use a fine brush to ease them between petals. Seal the tin and leave for 48 hours. When drying wired material, make sure the container is large enough to accommodate the "stems".*

Preserving with glycerine

This technique depends on replacing the plant's water with glycerine to keep the plant in a stable condition over a long period. Although a few flowers can be preserved in this way, for the most part foliage is better suited to the treatment. Its advantage is that the plant material remains supple, and therefore tends to look more natural; its disadvantage is that it causes dramatic color changes, plant material usually becoming dark brown or khaki.

For strong-stemmed material, make a solution of 40 per cent glycerine to 60 per cent hot water. Stand the stems in about 4 inches of the solution, making sure that the container supports the stems. Leave in

a cool, dark place for at least six days. Foliage is ready when small beads of glycerine start to form on the upper parts of the plant material. Remove from the solution and wash thoroughly.

To treat individual leaves in this way, make a stronger solution of 50 per cent glycerine to 50 per cent water. Leaves will absorb the glycerine they need in about six days.

SUITABLE PLANTS
Stemmed material: copper beech, elaeagnus, hydrangea, laurel, moluccella
Leaves: aspidistra, choisya, eucalyptus, holly, magnolia, mahonia, pin oak

---

Preserving strong-stemmed material

1 *Remove leaves and branches from the lower stems. Slit woody stem ends upwards for 2 inches. Finally, cut the stems at a sharp, diagonal angle.*

2 *Stand in the solution, making sure that hollow stems are supported by wire (see p. 190) and leave in a cool, dark place for 6–10 days.*

Preserving foliage

1 *Immerse single leaves or sprigs in solution, and leave in a dark place.*

2 *When the leaves have darkened, remove and wash in soapy water. Lay flat to dry.*

Coloring dried or preserved material

Many festive arrangements benefit from the inclusion of some brightly colored dried-plant material, and you can enliven much tired-looking material enormously by coloring it. There are several methods of coloring plant material.

Material preserved in glycerine

If you add dye to a glycerine solution (see p. 201), the plant material will drink the dye at the same time as the solution. Since foliage often turns a rather muddy color once it has absorbed glycerine, this is a good way to alter its drab appearance. Green dye, for example, will result in leaves that are darker than fresh ones, but they will certainly be more attractive than undyed ones.

You can also add artificial colours to foliage in this way. Red dye will give leaves such as eucalyptus an autumnal glow, while rust dye adds a warm, mellow look to lime bracts and copper beech leaves.

Alternatively, adding bleach to the glycerine solution will leave the plant material a creamy color.

Dyeing material as it air dries

If you are standing material in water before letting it air dry, you could add some dye to the water. The material will then drink the dye with the water before it starts to dry. For most purposes, it is best that the plant material should look absolutely natural when dried, so try to dye it a color that actually exists in a variety of the plant that you are dyeing. In general, blue is the least satisfactory color often producing extremely unnatural-looking plants.

Color spraying and painting

Special spray paints for coloring both fresh and dried flowers are available in a huge range of colors. Some are particularly useful. Sea lavender, which dries to a gray-white, can be sprayed a natural-looking pale yellow or pink. A combination of the two will result in an attractive peach color.

Brighter color sprays or fast-drying paint are ideal for festive decorations where you want to create a splash of color. Poppy seedheads and love-in-a-mist seedheads look wonderful colored bright red, bright pink or rich green. Pine cones, nuts and the delicate umbels of lovage, Queen Anne's lace, coriander and fennel look great sprayed silver or gold and then dredged with glitter before the paint has dried, so that the sparkling crystals adhere well. However, for all-year-round arrangements it is best to use only colors that are less striking and more natural-looking.

Spray painting

Taking three or four stems at a time, spray poppy Seedheads thoroughly with a red paint for a cheerfully festive effect at any time of the year.

Glittering

Spray pine cones with silver paint. Then sprinkle glitter over them for extra sparkle to make an attractive table centerpiece or tree decoration for Christmas.

Storing dried and preserved material

If you are harvesting and drying or pressing your own material you will probably have periods of surplus. When you need to store material for many months, you must be careful about how you pack it.

Any flowers that are hanging in bunches from the ceiling to dry can simply be left hanging after they have dried, so long as they are hanging out of direct sunlight. Similarly, any material that you are drying in a cupboard can be left where it is.

The most usual method of storing dried plant material, however, is to pack it away in sealed cardboard boxes, which are then placed in a cool, dry place, preferably with some ventilation. Before packing dried material ensure that it is completely dry. If there is still some moisture in just one flower, rot will soon set in once the box is packed. The cardboard boxes used for taking fresh flowers to market are probably the most suitable.

Air-dried plant material needs to be held firmly in place so that no pressure is placed on flowerheads, leaves or seedheads. Layers of pleated tissue paper or newspaper can be used to ensure that each bunch is well protected from its neighbor. Very strong material, such as cones or artichoke heads, requires no special protection and is best laid in a box or basket and stored in a cool, dry place until required.

Glycerined material should be packed in the same way as air-dried material. However, on no account pack glycerined and air-dried material in the same box, as plant material that has been preserved with glycerine still retains a certain amount of moisture and will therefore spoil dried flowers and foliage immediately.

You can also store pressed material in much the same way. Place it in a box, layering it between sheets of blotting paper, newspaper or tissue paper.

Packing dried-flower bundles
Glycerine- and air-dried material can be packed in the same way, although on no account mix the two. Plant material has to be held in place so that no pressure is placed on flowerheads, leaves or seedheads. Wrap fragile bunches in tissue paper first, and then pack them so that the stalks of the plants on one layer are separated from the heads of the material on the next layer with strips of pleated tissue or newspaper.

Wrapping delicate bunches

1 *When storing bunches of delicate-headed flowers, such as roses, wrap each bunch carefully in newspaper or tissue paper before packing it in a box. This will help to reduce pressure from neighboring* material. *Roll a sheet of newspaper loosely around the bunch to form a cone shape. It is best to begin by folding the edge of the paper in once to make the cone of flowers more secure.*

2 *Tuck in the narrow end of the cone as you roll the newspaper and, when you have wrapped the bunch, secure it with adhesive tape or a small rubber band, making sure you put no pressure on the stems.*

Wrapping individual hydrangeas

1 *All types of hydrangea heads are particularly fragile once they have been dried, and it is important that they should be individually wrapped with great care so that the petals are not damaged before they are stored away, hanging singly. Begin by placing each flowerhead close to one edge of a large sheet of soft tissue paper.*

2 *Gently form the tissue paper into a loose cone around the stem and flower, taking great care not to crush the delicate flower head as you wrap it. Once the tissue paper is in position, secure it carefully but firmly, using a small piece of adhesive tape. Move the flowerhead as little as possible while you are wrapping and securing it.*

3 *Take a long piece of string or raffia and tie the cone about 4 inches from the bottom. Form a hanging loop with the remainder of the string or raffia and hang the flowerheads individually in a cool, dry, airy place until required. Your work will quickly be ruined if left in a damp atmosphere to store.*

Wrapping large seedheads

1 *To protect a delicate seedhead on a strong stem pleat a strip of tissue paper 7–8 inches wide and 2 feet long.*

2 *Hold the pleated tissue 2 inches below the seedhead and fan out the pleats carefully to form a ruff around the head.*

3 *Secure the tissue paper wrapping in position making a string or raffia tie just below the point where the protective paper ruff fans out at the top of the stem.*

4 *The individually wrapped seedheads should be stored standing upright in an empty container in a dry location. Take care not to overfill the container because the "parcels" should not touch one another.*

SUITABLE PLANTS
Bulrush, heracleum, onion, tall grasses such as pampas grass, grains.

· CHAPTER NINE ·

DIRECTORY OF FLOWERS AND FOLIAGE

There is an almost bewildering wealth of plant material for the flower arranger to choose from. Of course, some plants are unsuitable for arranging, maybe because of their size or possibly their prickly spines, and some will not dry well. The following pages set out a wide selection of the plants that can be used successfully. Each entry gives a brief description of the plant, the time of year when it is at its best, plus brief advice on how to prepare it for arranging. Additional details on the conditioning of fresh plant material appears on pages 192–5 and on drying and preserving material on pages 196–201.

Traditional herbaceous border
Clumps of lofty delphiniums claim the attention with a supporting cast of Alchemilla mollis, *with its clouds of tiny, soft lime-green flowers, and pale-pink shrub and climbing roses. Altogether sharper notes are struck by the small crimson shrub rose and the orange bracts just making an appearance on the* Euphorbia griffithii. *A low, relatively wide, well-established box hedge makes a wonderfully trim border in delightful contrast with the robust climbers on the wall behind.*

Acacia **Mimosa**
Trees with clusters of fragrant yellow flowers and gray-green, finely cut leaves. The flowering branches of mimosa air dry well, retaining excellent flower color.
AVAILABILITY Spring.
CONDITIONING (FRESH) Scrape, slit and recut stems and then stand in deep water and cover with plastic bag for a day.
PICKING FOR DRYING Spring.
DRYING METHODS Air dry by hanging.

Acanthus **Bear's breeches, oyster plant**
Herbaceous plants with tall spikes of mauve, purple/white hooded flowers, with large, handsome glossy leaves. Long lasting in water.
AVAILABILITY Late summer.
CONDITIONING (FRESH) Slit and recut stems. Dip stem ends in boiling water and stand in deep water for three to four hours.
PICKING FOR DRYING Autumn.
DRYING METHODS Air dry flowers by hanging.

Acer **Maple**
Trees with green, yellow, brown and purple foliage, plus good autumn tints. Some maples are very slow growing and therefore unsuitable for repeated cutting. Some have excellent foliage and fragrant flowers in spring.
AVAILABILITY Summer for natural leaf colours; autumn for tints.
CONDITIONING (FRESH) Scrape, slit and recut stems and then stand in deep water for several hours. Float or submerge individual leaves for small arrangements.
PICKING FOR DRYING Summer and autumn.
DRYING METHODS Dry both summer and autumn foliage between newspaper in box. Press individual leaves in flower press.

Achillea **Yarrow**
Flat-headed, yellow flowers over a feathery foliage. Also pink/red and white varieties. *A. ptarmic* has white buttonlike flowers. All long lasting.
AVAILABILITY Summer, autumn.
CONDITIONING (FRESH) Slit and recut stems and then stand in deep water for several hours.
PICKING FOR DRYING Summer.
DRYING METHODS Air dry by hanging or by standing in container without water.

Acidanthera
White gladiolus-type flowers with dark blotches in the throat. Sweetly scented. Tall with thin, long leaves.
AVAILABILITY Early autumn.
CONDITIONING (FRESH) Stand in deep water for several hours.
PICKING FOR DRYING Early autumn.
DRYING METHODS Dry individual flowers in desiccant.

Aconitum **Monkshood**
Tall spikes of deep blue, hooded flowers. Also lighter blue, white and cream varieties. Poisonous.
AVAILABILITY Summer, autumn.
CONDITIONING (FRESH) Dip stem ends in boiling water or plug stem and then stand in deep water for several hours.
PICKING FOR DRYING Summer.
DRYING METHODS Air dry by hanging.

Aesculus **Horse chestnut**
Trees with "sticky buds" opening in water to reveal young leaves. Brown, shiny fruit, commonly known as "conkers". The huge leaves look good with clusters of the maturing fruit in large arrangements. Not suitable for drying.
AVAILABILITY Buds in spring; fruit in autumn.
CONDITIONING (FRESH) Scrape, slit and recut stems and stand in deep water for several hours.

Agapanthus **African lily, lily of the Nile**
Round globes of blue flowers in various shades. Also white varieties. Straplike leaves. Last quite well in water. Not suitable for drying.
AVAILABILITY Late summer to autumn.
CONDITIONING (FRESH) Stand in deep water for several hours.

Ajuga **Bugle**
Short ground-covering plants with spikes of blue flowers. There are varieties with pink flowers and also some with variegated or colored leaves. Medium lasting. Pretty in miniature arrangements. Not suitable for drying.
AVAILABILITY Spring and summer.
CONDITIONING (FRESH) Stand in deep water for several hours.

Alchemilla **Lady's mantle**
Feathery sprays of small, green-yellow flowers. Soft, round leaves holding pearls of water. Long lasting.
AVAILABILITY Spring to early autumn.
CONDITIONING (FRESH) Stand in deep water for several hours.
PICKING FOR DRYING Early summer.
DRYING METHODS Air dry by hanging. Mature flowers: preserve by standing in glycerine.

Allium **Onion family**
Bulbs producing round globes of purple or pink flowers. Also blue, white and yellow varieties. Long lasting. Dried, they can be used for their flower- or seedheads.
AVAILABILITY Spring and summer.
CONDITIONING (FRESH) Stand in deep water for several hours.
PICKING FOR DRYING Summer.
DRYING METHODS Air dry by hanging or standing in container without water or preserve seedheads by standing in glycerine.

Alstroemeria **Peruvian lily**
Trumpets of pink, red, orange, yellow and white flowers on longish stems. Good seed pods. Medium lasting.

AVAILABILITY Summer. All year from florists.

CONDITIONING (FRESH) Stand in deep water for several hours.

PICKING FOR DRYING Summer.

DRYING METHODS Air dry seedheads by hanging. Dry individual flowers with desiccant.

Althaea Hollyhock

Old-fashioned flowers with tall spikes of red, pink, purple, white or yellow. Grow in any conditions and have excellent seedheads.

AVAILABILITY Summer.

CONDITIONING (FRESH) Dip stem ends in boiling water and then stand in deep water for several hours before using.

PICKING FOR DRYING Summer.

DRYING METHODS Air dry seedheads by hanging. Dry individual single-varieties with desiccant.

Amaranthus
Love-lies-bleeding

Half-hardy annual plants with long ropes of crimson flowers. Also green variety available. Long lasting.

AVAILABILITY Summer, autumn.

CONDITIONING (FRESH) Remove most of the leaves and stand in deep water for several hours.

PICKING FOR DRYING Summer.

DRYING METHODS Air dry by hanging or standing in container without water or preserve by standing in glycerine. If dried hanging up, the tassel of the flowers dries straight. For a trailing effect, they should be dried upright.

Amaryllis Belladonna lily, naked lady

Bulbs with fragrant pink or white flowers on long stems, which can also be used as pot plants.

AVAILABILITY Autumn in gardens. Winter and spring from florists.

CONDITIONING (FRESH) Stand in deep water for several hours.

PICKING FOR DRYING Autumn.

DRYING METHODS Dry individual flowers with desiccant.

See also Hippeastrum.

Ammobium Winged everlasting, sandflower

These simple little white daisy flowers retain a good white when dried. They have thin stems near the flowerheads so wire bunches if you want them to stand upright, otherwise allow them to cascade on their own stems.

AVAILABILITY Summer.

CONDITIONING (FRESH) Stand in deep water for several hours.

PICKING FOR DRYING Summer.

DRYING METHODS Air dry by hanging.

Anaphalis Pearly everlasting

Silver-gray foliage plants that have small and white, yellow-centered flowers.

AVAILABILITY Summer, autumn.

CONDITIONING (FRESH) Stand in deep water for several hours before using.

PICKING FOR DRYING Summer before fully open.

DRYING METHODS Air dry by hanging or standing in container without water.

Anemone Windflower

There are several distinct anemones. First there are the spring-flowering types: blanda anemones which are short and delicate in shades of white, pink and blue; and the De Caen types, which are bright and in brash shades of red, blue and mauve. The autumn-flowering Japanese anemones are much taller and robust. These are white or pink.

AVAILABILITY Spring or autumn. De Caen are available from florists for most of the year.

CONDITIONING (FRESH) Stand in deep water for several hours.

PICKING FOR DRYING Spring and summer.

DRYING METHODS Press in flower press or dry individual flowerheads with desiccant.

Anethum Dill family

The white flowerheads form a delicate tracery in arrangements. Stems retain their aromatic scent for a considerable time.

AVAILABILITY Summer.

CONDITIONING (FRESH) Dip stem ends in boiling water and then stand in deep water for several hours.

PICKING FOR DRYING Summer.

DRYING METHODS Air dry by hanging.

Angelica

Large, white-green domes of flowers and bold foliage, usually found in herb gardens. Tall. Both flowers and seedheads good in arrangements.

AVAILABILITY Summer.

CONDITIONING (FRESH) Dip stem ends in boiling water and then stand in deep water for several hours.

DRYING METHODS Preserve seedheads by standing in glycerine.

Anigozanthos Kangaroo paw

Delicate cream trumpet flowers with rust- or yellow-colored calyx. Not suitable for fresh arrangements.

PICKING FOR DRYING Autumn.

DRYING METHODS Air dry by hanging.

Anthemis Chamomile

The small center of the white flower dries to a sturdy bobble. Try dying them a bright color. They are not suitable for fresh arrangements.

PICKING FOR DRYING Summer.

DRYING METHODS Air dry by hanging.

Anthriscus Chervil Family

Edible and decorative plants with large, flat heads of white flowers above delicate, lacy foliage. Last well but tend to exude a fine, sticky honeydew.

AVAILABILITY Spring.

CONDITIONING (FRESH) Dip stem ends in boiling water and then stand in deep water for several hours.

DRYING METHODS Air dry seedheads by hanging.

Anthurium

Exotic, greenhouse plants with heart-shaped leaves and a curious cylindrical flower coming from a bright heart-shaped bract. Five hundred species giving a large variety of color and shape. Very long lasting in water. Not suitable for drying.

AVAILABILITY Summer. All year from florists.

CONDITIONING (FRESH) Stand in deep water for several hours.

Antirrhinum Snapdragon

Annual bedding plants. Old-fashioned flowers with a good range of all colors except blue. The modern varieties are the best for arrangements. Short lasting in water. Not suitable for drying.

AVAILABILITY Summer.

CONDITIONING (FRESH) Stand in deep water for several hours.

Aquilegia Columbine

Old-fashioned cottage flowers. Short-lived in water but good as cut flowers because of the shape and variety of colors. All are suitable for cutting, but McKana hybrids are the best.

AVAILABILITY Summer.

CONDITIONING (FRESH) Stand in deep water for several hours.

PICKING FOR DRYING Summer.

DRYING METHODS Dry individual flowers with desiccant.

Arbutus Strawberry tree

Unusual trees in that the white flowers and the previous year's berries appear at the same time. The fruit look like strawberries. Not suitable for drying.

AVAILABILITY Late autumn.

CONDITIONING (FRESH) Scrape, slit and recut stems and then stand in deep water for several hours.

Armeria Thrift, sea pink

Cushions of short stems topped by a pink head of flowers. Deep pink and red varieties are available, but the leaves are of no

significance in arrangements. Quite a long life in water.

AVAILABILITY Summer.

CONDITIONING (FRESH) Stand in deep water for several hours.

PICKING FOR DRYING Summer.

DRYING METHODS Air dry by hanging.

Artemisia

Valuable for their tall stems of silvery gray foliage. Flowers insignificant except for A. lactiflora, which has green leaves and masses of small cream flowers. Long lasting in water.

AVAILABILITY Summer, autumn.

CONDITIONING (FRESH) Slit and recut stems. Dip stem ends in boiling water and then stand in deep water for several hours before arranging.

PICKING FOR DRYING Summer.

DRYING METHODS Air dry by hanging.

Arum

Native plants useful for their shiny spring foliage. A. italicum 'Pictum' is valuable as it has leaves with cream marbling throughout the winter. The spikes of red berries, although useful, are poisonous. Not suitable for drying.

AVAILABILITY Leaves: winter and spring. Berries: autumn.

CONDITIONING (FRESH) Submerge leaves in water for half an hour. Secure stems at top and bottom with rubber bands to prevent splitting and stand in deep water for an hour.

Arundinaria Bamboo

Slender stems with grasslike leaves. Rarely flowers. Bamboo dries easily and its leaves turn a blueish green.

AVAILABILITY All year.

CONDITIONING (FRESH) Two or three minutes in boiling vinegar to prevent leaves from curling, then stand in deep water for several hours.

PICKING FOR DRYING Summer.

DRYING METHODS Air dry by

standing in a container without water or lying flat, or preserve by standing in glycerine.

Asparagus

Valuable for the spikes or spears when they first appear, or tall fine, feathery foliage later on. In autumn they carry red berries, but the leaves drop readily once they start yellowing.

AVAILABILITY Spears: early summer. Foliage: summer and throughout year from florists.

CONDITIONING (FRESH) Stand in deep water for several hours.

PICKING FOR DRYING Summer.

DRYING METHODS Press foliage in flower press.

Aster Michaelmas daisy

A good range of tall, brightly colored daisies. There are many cultivars available and also more delicate species with airy sprays of small flowers. They last very well in water.

AVAILABILITY Autumn.

CONDITIONING (FRESH) Slit and recut stems and then stand in deep water for several hours.

PICKING FOR DRYING Autumn.

DRYING METHODS Press flowers in flower press.

See also Callistephus.

Astilbe Goat's beard

Tapering plumes of feathery flowers in a range of colors from pink through mauves to red as well as white and cream. Lots of varieties. The leaves are also very decorative. Not long lasting in water. Worth cutting after brown seedheads have formed.

AVAILABILITY Summer. Seedheads: Autumn.

CONDITIONING (FRESH) Stand in deep water for several hours.

PICKING FOR DRYING Summer.

DRYING METHODS Air dry by hanging. Press leaves in flower press.

Astrantia Masterwort

Curiously shaped greenish white flowers, each like a little posy.

There are shell pink and red forms, which grow to a medium height with good foliage. Last well in water. Combine well in arrangements with phlox and larkspur.
AVAILABILITY Summer, autumn.
CONDITIONING (FRESH) Stand in deep water for several hours.
PICKING FOR DRYING Summer.
DRYING METHODS Air dry by hanging.

Athyrium **Lady fern, female fern**
The green graceful fronds of lady fern look beautiful when used as a background to flowers or when featured with other foliage.
AVAILABILITY Summer.
CONDITIONING (FRESH) Dip stem ends in boiling water and then stand in deep water for several hours.
PICKING FOR DRYING Summer.
DRYING METHODS Press, either between newspaper under carpet where there is no traffic or alternatively in a flower press.

Aucuba
Shrubs that are useful for their all-year-round shiny green foliage. Variegated forms are available. Female plants also carry brilliant red berries. Not suitable for drying.
AVAILABILITY Foliage: all year. Berries: autumn and winter.
CONDITIONING (FRESH) Scrape, slit and recut stems and then stand in deep water for several hours.

Avena **Oats**
The delicate nodding heads of oats can be dried in their unripened green state or their ripened state, when they will be honey-colored.
AVAILABILITY Summer.
CONDITIONING (FRESH) Stand in deep water for several hours.
PICKING FOR DRYING Summer.
DRYING METHODS Air dry by hanging or standing in container without water.

Azalea
A type of *Rhododendron* with brightly colored flowers. They can be used as cut flowers or dwarf varieties can be grown in pots for display. Many cultivars are available; some are particularly fragrant, or have variegated flowers. None of them last long in water.
AVAILABILITY Spring, winter in pots if forced.
CONDITIONING (FRESH) Scrape, slit and recut stems. Dip stem ends in boiling water and then stand in deep water for several hours.
PICKING FOR DRYING Spring.
DRYING METHODS Press individual flowers in flower press.

Ballota
Perennials or sub-shrubs valuable for their furry, circular leaves, which are cupped around the arching stems. The hairs give the leaves a grayish green appearance. The flowers are insignificant. Last very well in water.
AVAILABILITY Summer, autumn.
CONDITIONING (FRESH) Dip stem ends in boiling water and then stand in deep water, not submerging the leaves.
PICKING FOR DRYING Summer and autumn.
DRYING METHODS Preserve by standing in glycerine (removing leaves after flowering) or air dry by hanging.

Banksia
Australian evergreen trees and shrubs with dramatic cones of yellow or red flowers. Tender and can only be grown in conservatories or greenhouses except in very mild areas.
AVAILABILITY Summer.
CONDITIONING (FRESH) Scrape, slit and recut stems and then stand in deep water for several hours.
PICKING FOR DRYING Spring.
DRYING METHODS Air dry by hanging.

Berberis **Barberry**
Spiny shrubs with green or purple foliage and yellow or orange flowers. Red berries are particularly useful in autumn. Not suitable for drying.
AVAILABILITY Foliage: spring to autumn, some species all year. Flowers: spring. Berries: autumn.
CONDITIONING (FRESH) Remove lower thorns. Scrape, slit and recut stems and then stand in deep water for several hours.

Bergenia
Large fleshy-leaved plants with drooping spikes of varying shades of pink flowers. Both leaves and flowers are good for fresh arrangements. Not suitable for drying.
AVAILABILITY Flowers: spring. Leaves: all year.
CONDITIONING (FRESH) Stand in deep water for several hours.

Betula **Birch**
These trees produce graceful bare branches in winter or sprays of fresh green leaves in spring. They also have small catkins in spring and catkinlike seed in autumn, the latter dropping badly. There are many forms of birch with varying bark color and leaf size. Color dried twigs for use in Christmas decorations and arrangements or use to make a wreath base.
AVAILABILITY Branches: all year. Leaves: spring, summer.
CONDITIONING (FRESH) Scrape, slit and recut stems and then stand in deep water for several hours.
PICKING FOR DRYING Winter.
DRYING METHODS Air dry twigs and branches in arrangement.

Bouvardia
Tender greenhouse shrubs with tight heads of tubular flowers in pink, white and yellow. Some species are fragrant. Not suitable for drying.
CONDITIONING (FRESH) Slit and

recut stems, dip stem ends in boiling water and stand in deep water for several hours.

Brassica **Cabbage family**
Many brassicas are very decorative, not only the round leafy varieties, but the tall spires of Brussels sprouts, white and purple buds of the broccolis, the white curds of cauliflowers and the curly leaves of kale. Both cabbages and Brussels have red forms. There are also brightly colored ornamental cabbages. Not suitable for drying.
AVAILABILITY Cabbages: all year. Brussels: autumn and winter. Ornamentals: autumn.
CONDITIONING (FRESH) Submerge leaves for half an hour then stand in water for another half hour.

Briza **Quaking grass**
Graceful grasses with drooping compact heads which move in the slightest draft. Pale green when fresh. Quite unlike any other grass in shape. Long-lasting and make a good filler in an arrangement.
AVAILABILITY Summer, autumn.
CONDITIONING (FRESH) None.
PICKING FOR DRYING Summer.
DRYING METHODS Air dry by standing in container without water or hanging.

Brodiaea
Bulbous plants similar to the decorative allium. Blue or purple heads on medium stems. Leaves often shrivel before flower opens, so of no consequence.
AVAILABILITY Summer.
CONDITIONING (FRESH) Stand in deep water for several hours.
PICKING FOR DRYING Summer.
DRYING METHODS Press individual flowers in flower press.

Brunnera
These herbaceous plants have myriad pale-blue flowers floating above the heart-shaped leaves. Not very tall. Last reasonably well in water.

AVAILABILITY Early summer.
CONDITIONING (FRESH) Slit and recut stems then stand in deep water for several hours.
PICKING FOR DRYING Early summer.
DRYING METHODS Press sprays of flowers in flower press.

Buddleia **Butterfly bush**
Fragrant shrubs with long spikes of mauve, purple or white flowers. Also species with globes of orange or yellow flowers. The gray-silver or green foliage should be removed as it does not last well. Not suitable for drying.
AVAILABILITY Spring, summer and autumn.
CONDITIONING (FRESH) Dip stem ends in boiling water and then stand in deep water for several hours.

Bupleurum sp.
This tender, semi evergreen Australian plant makes a good background filler, both for its green foliage and small white flowerheads.
AVAILABILITY Summer, autumn.
CONDITIONING (FRESH) Slit and recut stems and then stand in deep water for several hours.
PICKING FOR DRYING Mid to late summer.
DRYING METHODS Air dry flowers by hanging.

Buxus **Box**
Evergreen shrubs with small glossy leaves. Last a very long time in water. Also variegated variety available. Flowers of no consequence.
AVAILABILITY All year.
CONDITIONING (FRESH) Scrape, slit and recut stems and then stand in water for several hours.
PICKING FOR DRYING All year.
DRYING METHODS Preserve by standing in glycerine.

Caladium **Angel wings**
Tender pot plants grown for their foliage. The large, heart-shaped leaves have veins of a contrasting

color. The leaves can be green, white, cream or pale pink. They do not last long if cut. Not suitable for drying.
AVAILABILITY Summer.
CONDITIONING (FRESH) Submerge leaves in water for half an hour before using.

Calendula **Pot marigold**
Hardy annuals with bright-yellow or vibrant orange flowers. Old-fashioned, cottage flowers. They last quite well in water.
AVAILABILITY Summer.
CONDITIONING (FRESH) Stand in deep water for several hours.
PICKING FOR DRYING Summer.
DRYING METHODS Air dry quickly by hanging in a warm cupboard or warm oven. Press individual flowers in flower press.

Callistemon **Bottlebrush tree**
Half-hardy and tender trees from Australia with beautiful bright red or yellow flowers with spikes of stamens that closely resemble bottle brushes. Bottle-brush provides one of the best reds of any dried flower.
AVAILABILITY Summer.
CONDITIONING (FRESH) Scrape, slit and recut stems and then stand in deep water for several hours.
PICKING FOR DRYING Summer.
DRYING METHODS Air dry flowers by hanging.

Callistephus **China aster**
Daisylike annuals available in a wide range of bright colors. Come in singles or doubles. Last well in water.
AVAILABILITY Autumn.
CONDITIONING (FRESH) Stand in deep water for several hours.
PICKING FOR DRYING Late summer and autumn.
DRYING METHODS Press individual flowers in flower press or dry in desiccant.

Camassia **Quamash**
Bulbs producing long stems with spikes of large, star-shaped

flowers in blue or white. They do not last very long in water but are valuable for their blue color. Allow the seedheads to dry on the plant.
AVAILABILITY Summer.
CONDITIONING (FRESH) Stand in deep water for several hours.
PICKING FOR DRYING Flowers: summer.
DRYING METHODS Dry individual flowers in desiccant.

Camellia
Superb white, pink or red flowers set against glossy green leaves. There are many hardy cultivars to choose from. Long lasting in water.
AVAILABILITY Late winter and spring. Earlier from florists.
CONDITIONING (FRESH) Scrape, slit and recut stems and then stand in deep water for several hours.
PICKING FOR DRYING Flowers: spring. Leaves: summer.
DRYING METHODS Flowers: dry with desiccant or crystallize. Leaves: preserve by standing in glycerine.

Campanula Bellflower
A vast range of blue flowers from very short to tall, the shorter having single bells, the taller whole spikes of flowers. Very cool in appearance. White forms are also available. They last well in water.
AVAILABILITY Summer.
CONDITIONING (FRESH) Stand in deep water for several hours.
PICKING FOR DRYING Summer.
DRYING METHODS Press individual flowers in flower press.

Capsicum Pepper
Green or bright red fruit with shiny skins producing good highlights in arrangements. Purchased fruit do not last as long as home-produced. Dried peppers tend to shrivel, although they keep a good color.
AVAILABILITY Autumn or all year from produce markets.

CONDITIONING (FRESH) Polish.
PICKING FOR DRYING Autumn.
DRYING METHODS Air dry by hanging.

Carlina Carline thistle
These beautiful, but vicious, large flower thistles, 4–5 inches across, are one of the strongest-looking dried flowers and, although they have a wild look about them, they suit both formal and informal arrangements. Their prickles, however, make them unsuitable for fresh arrangements.
PICKING FOR DRYING Autumn.
DRYING METHODS Air dry by standing in container without water.

Carthamus Safflower
Pick just as the orange petals begin to show for best dried results. The flower color is strong and safflower will show well if arranged in groups. It is worth drying safflower with the upper leaves on the stem, as they provide an excellent foil for the flowers.
AVAILABILITY Summer.
CONDITIONING (FRESH) Stand in deep water for several hours.
PICKING FOR DRYING Summer.
DRYING METHODS Air dry by hanging.

Castanea Chestnut
Good, large-leaved foliage; fluffy yellow flowers (some might not like the smell) and then light green, spiny fruit cases in autumn, opening to reveal shiny brown nuts.
AVAILABILITY Leaves: spring and summer. Flowers: summer. Fruit cases and nuts: autumn.
CONDITIONING (FRESH) Scrape, slit and recut stems and then stand in deep water for several hours. Polish nuts.
PICKING FOR DRYING Spring and summer.
DRYING METHODS Preserve leaves standing in glycerine. Dry nuts in basket.

Catananche Cupid's dart
Pale-blue, dark-eyed flowers with a papery calyx on thin stems. Very long lasting in water or as dried flowers.
AVAILABILITY Summer, autumn.
CONDITIONING (FRESH) Stand in deep water for several hours.
PICKING FOR DRYING Summer.
DRYING METHODS Air dry by hanging, press in flower press or dry in desiccant.

Cattleya
A wonderful range of epiphytic orchids with broad lips. The largest flowers can be up to 10 inches across. Many species and cultivars are available giving a good range of colors with purple predominating. Some are fragrant. Short-stemmed and delicate. Not suitable for drying.
AVAILABILITY All year.
CONDITIONING (FRESH) Stand in deep water for several hours.

Ceanothus
Evergreen and deciduous shrubs with fluffy round clusters of varying shades of blue flowers. The evergreen varieties have particularly good foliage. Not suitable for drying.
AVAILABILITY Summer and early autumn.
CONDITIONING (FRESH) Scrape, slit and recut stems and then stand in deep water for several hours.

Celosia
Spectacular plants with bright red or yellow feathery plumes.
AVAILABILITY Late summer and autumn.
CONDITIONING (FRESH) Dip stem ends in boiling water and then stand in deep water for several hours.
PICKING FOR DRYING Summer.
DRYING METHODS Air dry by hanging.

Centaurea Cornflower
Long-lasting annuals. The basic color is blue but there is now a

good range available including white, pink, mauve and red. The related species sweet sultan (*C. moschata*) has deliciously fragrant flowers.

AVAILABILITY Summer.

CONDITIONING (FRESH) Stand in deep water for several hours.

PICKING FOR DRYING Summer.

DRYING METHODS Air dry by hanging or dry in desiccant.

Centranthus Valerian

Large heads of deep-pink or red flowers with fleshy stems and foliage. There are also white forms available. None is suitable for drying.

AVAILABILITY Summer.

CONDITIONING (FRESH) Dip ends of young stems in boiling water. Stand in deep water for several hours.

Chaenomeles Flowering quince

Waxy, apple-blossom type flowers clustered tight to the leafless branches. Mainly shades of red but also white and pink. Bears curiously colored orange fruit in autumn.

AVAILABILITY Flowers: spring. Fruit: autumn.

CONDITIONING (FRESH) Scrape, slit and recut stems and then stand in deep water for several hours.

PICKING FOR DRYING Spring.

DRYING METHODS Press flowers in flower press.

Chaerophyllum

The flowering umbels of this and most similar umbelliferous plants, such as fennel, dill, and Queen Anne's lace can be pressed to form beautiful radiating patterns of stems and flowers. The seedheads can also be dried successfully.

PICKING FOR DRYING Summer.

DRYING METHODS Flowers: press or air dry by hanging or standing in container without water. Seedheads: air dry by hanging or standing.

Chamaerops Dwarf fan palm

Trunkless palm trees. Leaves are fanlike with between 12 and 15 blades. The leaf stalks are spiny. Last very well when cut.

AVAILABILITY All year.

CONDITIONING (FRESH) Stand in deep water for several hours.

PICKING FOR DRYING All year.

DRYING METHODS Air dry by hanging.

Cheiranthus Wallflower

The well-known wallflowers come in a wide range of colors except blue. They are fragrant and last very well in water.

AVAILABILITY Spring.

CONDITIONING (FRESH) Slit and recut stems and then stand in deep water for several hours. It may be necessary to dip stem ends in boiling water.

PICKING FOR DRYING Spring.

DRYING METHODS Press individual flowers in flower press.

Chenopodium

The large flowering stems of this native plant dry easily. Use the flowering side spikes as a filler, or whole stems for dramatic impact in large arrangements.

AVAILABILITY Summer.

CONDITIONING (FRESH) Dip stem ends in boiling water and then stand in deep water for several hours.

PICKING FOR DRYING Autumn.

DRYING METHODS Air dry in container without water.

Chionodoxa Glory of the snow

Short-stemmed bulbs with delightful starry flowers, blue or pink with a white throat.

AVAILABILITY Spring.

CONDITIONING (FRESH) Stand in deep water for several hours.

PICKING FOR DRYING Spring.

DRYING METHODS Press in flower press.

Choisya Mexican orange blossom

Clusters of fragrant white flowers surrounded by glossy leaves forming a natural nosegay. The foliage is valuable in its own right for arrangements. Leaves are ideal for preserving in glycerine; they turn a soft shade of cream.

AVAILABILITY Flowers: summer. Foliage: all year.

CONDITIONING (FRESH) Scrape, slit and recut stems and then stand in deep water for several hours.

PICKING FOR DRYING Summer.

DRYING METHODS Preserve leaves by standing in glycerine.

Chrysanthemum

One of the most popular cut flowers with their large range of shapes and warm colors. They last a very long time in water. Some people do not like the smell of the bruised foliage. Also available as pot plants. Most chrysanthemums will not dry but *C. vulgare* air dries well.

AVAILABILITY Autumn. All year from florists.

CONDITIONING (FRESH) Slit and recut stems and then stand in deep water for several hours.

PICKING FOR DRYING Summer.

DRYING METHODS Air dry by hanging. Press single flowers in flower press; dry double blooms in desiccant.

Cimifuga Black snake root

Long heads, almost like extended bottle brushes, with white or cream flowers. The long stems are a rich dark-brown. Some have ferny leaves. Last reasonably well in water. Not suitable for drying.

AVAILABILITY Summer, autumn.

CONDITIONING (FRESH) Dip stem ends in boiling water and then stand in deep water for several hours.

Cladonia sp. Silver lichen

Lichen is extremely versatile and is used either dry or fresh. Can be used as a base for dried-flower arrangements or as exterior cladding for wreaths, trees or

any other shape. Alternatively, separate pieces can be wired and used like flowers. Conditioning not necessary for fresh arrangements.
PICKING FOR DRYING Any time.
DRYING METHODS Air dry in a box or basket.

Clarkia Godetia
Easy-to-grow annuals with brightly colored flowers like funnels of crêpe paper in pink, red, purple, orange and white. Some of the flowers are semi-double or double. Leaves insignificant. Cut flowers last well in water.
AVAILABILITY Late spring, summer and autumn.
CONDITIONING (FRESH) Dip stem ends in boiling water and then stand in deep water for several hours.
PICKING FOR DRYING Summer.
DRYING METHODS Dry individual flowers in desiccant.

Clematis
Climbing and herbaceous plants. The smaller varieties make ideal trailing displays while the larger flowered varieties can be used singly. The herbaceous varieties last better in water. Seedheads are also valuable for use in arrangements.
AVAILABILITY Spring, summer and autumn. Seedheads: autumn.
CONDITIONING (FRESH) Slit and recut stems. Dip stem ends in boiling water and then stand in deep water for several hours.
PICKING FOR DRYING Late summer.
DRYING METHODS Air dry seedheads by hanging. Press flowers in flower press.

Clivia
Round heads of trumpet-shaped flowers in red and orange. Strap-shaped, glossy, dark-green leaves. Last well in water.
AVAILABILITY Spring.
CONDITIONING (FRESH) Stand in

deep water for several hours.
PICKING FOR DRYING Spring.
DRYING METHODS Dry individual flowers in desiccant.

Cobaea Cup and saucer vine
Annual or perennial climbing plants with large bell-shaped flowers of purple or pale green.
AVAILABILITY Summer, autumn.
CONDITIONING (FRESH) Stand in deep water for several hours.
PICKING FOR DRYING Summer and early autumn.
DRYING METHODS Dry individual flowers in desiccant.

Conifers
A wide range of evergreen trees and shrubs to give all-year foliage for decoration. The cones are also decorative in some species.
AVAILABILITY All year.
CONDITIONING (FRESH) Slit and recut stems then stand in deep water for several hours.
PICKING FOR DRYING All year.
DRYING METHODS Pick fresh and then dry in arrangements, or preserve foliage by standing in glycerine.

Convallaria Lily-of-the-valley
Delicate little sprays of white bells of great charm. Excellent fragrance. A pink variety available. Good backing foliage. Last well in water.
AVAILABILITY Spring. Forced: all year.
CONDITIONING (FRESH) Stand in deep water for several hours.
PICKING FOR DRYING Spring.
DRYING METHODS Press flowers in flower press or dry in desiccant.

Coreopsis Tickseed
Yellow daisylike flowers with darker yellow eyes. They generally have long stems and deeply divided leaves. Several cultivars available with different shades of yellow and varying sizes of head and height.
AVAILABILITY Summer.
CONDITIONING (FRESH) Stand in

deep water for several hours.
PICKING FOR DRYING Summer.
DRYING METHODS Press flowers in flower press or dry in desiccant.

Cornus Dogwood
A large range of shrubs with good bark for winter arrangements. White or yellow flowers and bracts in spring. Good tints in autumn.
AVAILABILITY Bark: all year, particularly winter. Flowers: spring. Tints: autumn.
CONDITIONING (FRESH) Scrape, slit and recut stems. Dip stem ends in boiling water and then stand in deep water for several hours.
PICKING FOR DRYING Summer and autumn.
DRYING METHODS Press individual leaves in flower press.

Cortaderia selloana Pampas grass
Pick pink or cream pampas plumes the moment they are fully formed and treat them with hair spray to prevent the seeds from dropping. Arrange by themselves, or with other grasses, or separate the sections of each plume and use in smaller arrangements.
AVAILABILITY Autumn.
CONDITIONING (FRESH) Stand in deep water for several hours.
PICKING FOR DRYING Autumn.
DRYING METHODS Air dry by standing in container with a little water or preserve by standing in glycerine.

Corydalis
A genus of plants becoming very popular but difficult to obtain except for C. lutea. Small, delicate yellow flowers over filigree foliage.
AVAILABILITY Summer.
CONDITIONING (FRESH) Stand in deep water for several hours.
PICKING FOR DRYING Summer.
DRYING METHODS Press flowers and foliage in flower press.

Corylus Hazel

The familiar yellow catkins or lambs' tails of the hedgerow and fields. The variety *C. avellana* 'Contorta' has delightful twisted stems. Also purple-leaved variety which is good for foliage. Dried branches can be colored for use in festive decorations and arrangements.
AVAILABILITY Catkins: late winter, spring. Foliage: spring, summer.
CONDITIONING (FRESH) Slit and recut stems then stand in water for several hours.
PICKING FOR DRYING Winter.
DRYING METHODS Catkins: air dry by hanging or preserve by standing in glycerine. Stems: as for fresh and then air dry in position.

Cosmos

Tall fresh-looking plants with feathery foliage and flowers of white, pink, red and orange. *C. atrosanguineus* has unusually dark brown flowers and a smell reminiscent of hot chocolate. Last quite well in water.
AVAILABILITY Summer, autumn.
CONDITIONING (FRESH) Stand in deep water for several hours.
PICKING FOR DRYING Summer and autumn.
DRYING METHODS Press flowers and foliage in flower press.

Cotinus Smoke bush

Very valuable shrubs or trees with beautiful purple foliage. The leaves have a simple rounded shape which can be used to form a good background in arrangement. Also have good autumn tints. All varieties last reasonably well in water.
AVAILABILITY Summer, autumn.
CONDITIONING (FRESH) Scrape, slit and recut stems. Dip stem ends in boiling water and then stand in deep water for several hours.
PICKING FOR DRYING Autumn.
DRYING METHODS Air dry by hanging or press individual leaves in flower press.

Crocosmia Montbretia

Tall bulbous plants with sword-like leaves and arching sprays of bright orange flowers. Yellow varieties also available. Last quite well in water.
AVAILABILITY Late summer and autumn.
CONDITIONING (FRESH) Stand in deep water for several hours.
PICKING FOR DRYING Summer.
DRYING METHODS Seed pods: air dry by hanging. Flowers: dry in desiccants or press in flower press.

Crocus

Small bulbous plants bearing flowers shaped like chalices. Colors vary from cream and bright orange to blue and mauve. Also autumn forms. Before drying, wire each flower.
AVAILABILITY Late winter, spring and autumn.
CONDITIONING (FRESH) Stand in deep water for several hours.
PICKING FOR DRYING Early spring.
DRYING METHODS Dry with desiccant.

Cryptomeria Japanese cedar

Evergreen conifers with bronze, feathery foliage in winter and bright green foliage in spring. There are several varieties.
AVAILABILITY All year.
CONDITIONING (FRESH) Scrape, slit and recut stems and then stand in deep water for several hours.
PICKING FOR DRYING Summer.
DRYING METHODS As for fresh and then air dry in arrangement, or preserve by standing in glycerine. Air dry separate cones in a basket.

Cuphea

Small, drooping tubular flowers in a variety of bright reds and yellow. Suitable for tiny arrangements. Not suitable for drying.
AVAILABILITY Summer. Greenhouse: all year.
CONDITIONING (FRESH) Stand in deep water for several hours.

Cyclamen

A number of delicate species which will give almost all-year-round flowering in greenhouse and open garden. Also larger, more showy, florists' cyclamen as indoor houseplants. Colors available include white, mauve, pink and purple.
AVAILABILITY Species: autumn, winter and spring. Florists' plants: all year.
CONDITIONING (FRESH) Stand in deep water for several hours.
PICKING FOR DRYING All year.
DRYING METHODS Press smaller leaves in flower press.

Cymbidium

Aerial sprays of beautiful, exotic orchids in a large variety of colors with the exception of blue. They last extremely well in water.
AVAILABILITY All year from florists.
CONDITIONING (FRESH) Stand in deep water for several hours.
PICKING FOR DRYING All year.
DRYING METHODS Dry flowers in desiccant.

Cynara Globe artichoke

Versatile plants with good foliage and flowerheads. The latter are large and thistlelike and can be used in bud, in flower or in seed. The leaves are evergreen. The flowerheads can be dried.
AVAILABILITY Flowers: autumn. Leaves: all year.
CONDITIONING (FRESH) Stand in deep water for several hours.
PICKING FOR DRYING Flowers: summer. Bracts: autumn.
DRYING METHODS Air dry by hanging or standing in container without water.

Cyperus Papyrus, umbrella plant

Plants with leaflike bracts radiating from the top of the stem. Houseplants, but stems can be cut for arrangements. Last well in water.
AVAILABILITY Summer.

CONDITIONING (FRESH) Stand in deep water for several hours.
PICKING FOR DRYING Spring.
DRYING METHODS Air dry by hanging.

Cypripedium **Slipper orchid**
Curious orchids with slipperlike pouches, surmounted by waxed moustaches. Not so bright as some of the other orchids.
AVAILABILITY Summer.
CONDITIONING (FRESH) Stand in deep water for several hours.
PICKING FOR DRYING Summer.
DRYING METHODS Dry flowers in desiccant.

Cytisus **Broom**
Shrubs with masses of pealike blooms. Available in white, yellow, orange, pink and red.
AVAILABILITY Spring.
CONDITIONING (FRESH) Slit and recut stems. Dip stem ends in boiling water and then stand in deep water for several hours.
PICKING FOR DRYING Spring.
DRYING METHODS Stems (after flowers drop) air dry by hanging or preserve by standing in glycerine. Flowers: dry in desiccant.

Dahlia
Half-hardy tuberous plants with a great variety in flower shape and color. Colors include white, red, mauve, yellow and orange. Stems are long. They last well in water, especially pom-poms. For drying, pick about four days before flowers reach perfection.
AVAILABILITY Late summer and autumn.
CONDITIONING (FRESH) Stand in deep water for several hours.
PICKING FOR DRYING Autumn.
DRYING METHODS Air dry by hanging, or dry with desiccant.

Daphne
Small slow-growing shrubs with fragrant flowers mainly in red, purple and white, also some in yellow. *D. laureola* is evergreen. Not suitable for drying.

AVAILABILITY Late winter, spring and summer.
CONDITIONING (FRESH) Scrape, slit and recut stems. Dip stem ends in boiling water and then stand in deep water for several hours.

Delphinium
Tall spires of varying shades of spurred, blue flowers with a dark or white center. Also white, pink and purple varieties available. Dwarf forms can now also be found. They dry best in a cool, dark, dry place. Pick when two-thirds developed.
AVAILABILITY Summer, and sometimes second flush in autumn.
CONDITIONING (FRESH) Plug hollow stems with cotton ball and then stand in deep water for several hours.
PICKING FOR DRYING Summer.
DRYING METHODS Air dry flowers (remove leaves) by hanging or standing in container in a little water. Press individual flowers and small sprays of foliage in flower press.

Deutzia
Shrubs with clusters of small single or double flowers in white or pink. Some of the double flowers are delightfully fringed. Last quite well in water.
AVAILABILITY Late spring and summer.
CONDITIONING (FRESH) Scrape, slit and recut stems and then stand in deep water for several hours.
PICKING FOR DRYING Spring and summer.
DRYING METHODS Dry small sprays in desiccant.

Dianthus **Carnation, pink, sweet william**
One of the most popular of cut flowers. White, pink and red cultivars are available, some with a contrasting eye. Usually fragrant. All long lasting in water.
AVAILABILITY Summer and

autumn (old-fashioned pinks and sweet williams early summer only). All year from florists.
CONDITIONING (FRESH) Stand in deep water for several hours.
PICKING FOR DRYING Summer.
DRYING METHODS Air dry small double pinks by hanging. Dry carnations in desiccant. Press single pinks in flower press.

Dicentra **Bleeding heart**
Beautiful arching sprays of heart-shaped flowers with ferny foliage. Pink or white flowers. Last well in water.
AVAILABILITY Spring, summer.
CONDITIONING (FRESH) Stand in deep water for several hours.
PICKING FOR DRYING Spring and summer.
DRYING METHODS Press individual flowers in flower press or dry in desiccant.

Digitalis **Foxglove**
These tall spires of purple bells evoke high summer. There are varieties with bells all around the stems and other colors including white and yellow.
AVAILABILITY Summer.
CONDITIONING (FRESH) Dip stem ends in boiling water after removing longer leaves and then stand in deep water for several hours.
PICKING FOR DRYING Summer.
DRYING METHODS Air dry seed-heads by hanging. Dry individual flowers in desiccant.

Doronicum **Leopard's bane**
Golden yellow daisies that always seem to exude a fresh-ness when they first appear in spring. There are also double-flowered varieties.
AVAILABILITY Spring.
CONDITIONING (FRESH) Stand in deep water for several hours.
PICKING FOR DRYING Spring.
DRYING METHODS Press flowers in flower press.

Dryandra
Australian evergreen shrubs with orange and red flowers.

AVAILABILITY Spring.
CONDITIONING (FRESH) Scrape, slit and recut stems and then stand in water for several hours.
PICKING FOR DRYING Summer.
DRYING METHODS Air dry by hanging.

Dryopteris
Fern fronds press very easily and, because they grow in a two-dimensional way, they look perfectly natural when used pressed in arrangements.
AVAILABILITY Summer.
CONDITIONING (FRESH) Dip stem ends in boiling water and then stand in deep water for several hours.
PICKING FOR DRYING Summer.
DRYING METHODS Air dry flat or press between newspaper under carpet where there is no traffic.

Echinops **Globe thistle**
Popular border plants with spiny spherical flowers much loved by bees. The most common globe thistle has blue flowers but there are also light-green and white varieties. Tall and last very well in water. For drying, pick before the flower develops fully.
AVAILABILITY Summer.
CONDITIONING (FRESH) Stand in deep water for several hours. Dip stem ends of young stems in boiling water.
PICKING FOR DRYING Summer.
DRYING METHODS Air dry by hanging or preserve mature flowers in glycerine.

Echium **Viper's bugloss**
Wild plants sometimes grown in gardens. Coils of blue flowers with red stamens. The leaves and stems are covered with small spines that get into the hands. Cultivated garden hybrids give a greater range of colors. Not suitable for drying.
AVAILABILITY Summer.
CONDITIONING (FRESH) Dip stem ends in boiling water and then stand in deep water for several hours.

Elaeagnus
Evergreen shrubs valuable for their foliage. *E. pungens* 'Maculata' and *E.* × *ebbingei* 'Gilt Edge' have excellent gold and green foliage and *E. angustifolia* and *E. commutata* have good silver foliage. To preserve, add green dye to the glycerine to "help" the color.
AVAILABILITY All year.
CONDITIONING (FRESH) Hammer woody stems then stand in deep water for several hours.
PICKING FOR DRYING Summer.
DRYING METHODS Preserve by standing in glycerine.

Epilobium **Willow herb**
Wild or garden plants with spires of dark rosy-red flowers. Some species have very tall stems. Wild forms can be invasive if grown in the garden.
AVAILABILITY Summer.
CONDITIONING (FRESH) Dip stem ends in boiling water and then stand in deep water for several hours. Wilt unless dealt with right after picking.
PICKING FOR DRYING Summer.
DRYING METHODS Press individual flowers in flower press.

Eremurus **Foxtail lily**
Very tall, airy spikes of starlike flowers. Colors are white, pink or yellow. Some species are fragrant. Last well in water.
AVAILABILITY Summer.
CONDITIONING (FRESH) Stand in deep water for several hours.
PICKING FOR DRYING Summer.
DRYING METHODS Press individual flowers in flower press or dry in desiccant.

Erica **Heath**
Small shrubby plants useful both for the color of their flowers and their foliage. There are always some varieties in flower all year. Flower color varies from white to pink, mauve and purple. The leaves are of varying shades of green and gold. Even the rust brown seedheads are attractive.

AVAILABILITY All year.
CONDITIONING (FRESH) Slit and recut stems and then stand in deep water for several hours.
PICKING FOR DRYING Summer.
DRYING METHODS Air dry by standing in container in a little water.

Erodium
Small, geraniumlike flowers in pink and white varieties. The leaves and flowers press well.
AVAILABILITY Summer.
CONDITIONING (FRESH) Stand in deep water for several hours.
PICKING FOR DRYING Summer.
DRYING METHODS Press in flower press.

Eryngium **Sea holly**
Very spiky but very decorative plants in which even the flowers have spines. Colors are mainly blue but there are also green and white varieties. Some are a very airy maze of branches, others are more compact.
AVAILABILITY Summer, autumn.
CONDITIONING (FRESH) Stand in deep water for several hours.
PICKING FOR DRYING Late summer.
DRYING METHODS Air dry by hanging or preserve by standing in glycerine.

Escallonia
Late-flowering shrubs with arching stems covered with clusters of starry flowers in shades of pink, red and white. Glossy evergreen foliage. Last quite well in water.
AVAILABILITY Late summer and autumn.
CONDITIONING (FRESH) Scrape, slit and recut stems and then stand in deep water for several hours.
PICKING FOR DRYING Summer and autumn.
DRYING METHODS Flowers: dry in desiccant or press in flower press. Leaves: preserve by standing in glycerine.

Eucalyptus **Gum tree**
Very valuable for their evergreen grayish silver foliage. Their very airy white flowers can also be attractive in arrangements. Long lasting in water.
AVAILABILITY Foliage: all year. Flowers: late autumn, early winter.
CONDITIONING (FRESH) Scrape, slit and recut stems and then stand in deep water for several hours.
PICKING FOR DRYING Summer.
DRYING METHODS Air dry by hanging, or preserve by standing in glycerine.

Euonymus **Spindle**
The deciduous spindles are valuable for their autumn color and their red berries which open like a cardinal's hat. The evergreens are valuable for their glossy foliage of which there are good variegated forms. Not suitable for drying.
AVAILABILITY Autumn for tints and berries. All year for evergreen foliage.
CONDITIONING (FRESH) Scrape, slit and recut stems and then stand in deep water for several hours.

Euphorbia **Spurge**
Valuable yellow- and green-leaved plants varying in height from short to tall. Long lasting in water. They also include the red-bracted house plant poinsettia. Exude a caustic white sap. Not suitable for drying.
AVAILABILITY Spring and summer. Winter for poinsettia.
CONDITIONING (FRESH) Staunch the sap with a naked flame or fine sand. Stand in deep water for several hours.

Eustoma **Prairie gentian**
Beautiful trumpets of delicately arching purple flowers.
AVAILABILITY Summer only, from florists.
CONDITIONING (FRESH) Dip stem ends in boiling water and then stand in deep water for several hours.
DRYING METHODS Dry flowers in desiccant.

Fagus **Beech**
Valuable shiny foliage in either green or purple. The nut capsules are an interesting shape and can also be useful.
AVAILABILITY Foliage: spring and summer. Fruit: autumn.
CONDITIONING (FRESH) Scrape, slit and recut stems and then stand in deep water for several hours. Dip ends of young stems in boiling water.
PICKING FOR DRYING Summer.
DRYING METHODS Air dry flat or press between newspaper under carpet where there is no traffic or preserve by standing in glycerine. Air dry nuts in basket.

Fatsia **Japanese aralia**
Large, glossy, dark green leaves, deeply lobed like the fingers on a hand. Valuable for foliage decorations. Long lasting in water. Leaves preserved in glycerine become dark brown.
AVAILABILITY Summer.
CONDITIONING (FRESH) Slit and recut stems and then stand in deep water for several hours.
PICKING FOR DRYING Summer.
DRYING METHODS Air dry flat or press between newspaper under carpet where there is no traffic or preserve by standing in glycerine.

Ferns
A wide range of shapes and textures; some filigree, others straplike. The fronds also have quite a range of different greens. They last well in water once they are cut.
AVAILABILITY Spring to autumn.
CONDITIONING (FRESH) Char stem ends with small flame and stand in deep water for several hours. Dip ends of young stems in boiling water.
PICKING FOR DRYING Spring and summer.

DRYING METHODS Air dry flat or press between newspaper under carpet where there is no traffic.

Ficus **Rubber plant, weeping fig**
Foliage plants with glossy, leathery leaves of different sizes. Some useful for cutting. Not suitable for drying.
AVAILABILITY All year.
CONDITIONING (FRESH) Dip stem ends in boiling water and then stand in water for several hours.

Foeniculum **Fennel**
The delicate seed formation of fennel looks much like dill when dry and can be used for its feathery texture.
AVAILABILITY Summer.
CONDITIONING (FRESH) Dip stem ends in boiling water and then stand in water for several hours.
PICKING FOR DRYING Summer
DRYING METHODS Air dry by hanging or preserve seedheads by standing in glycerine.

Forsythia
Shrubs with starry yellow flowers which are out just before the leaves appear. Can be cut in winter for forcing long before the flowers normally appear. Last quite well in water.
AVAILABILITY Spring. Winter if forced.
CONDITIONING (FRESH) Scrape, slit and recut stems and then stand in deep water for several hours. Dip stem ends in boiling water to force flowers.
PICKING FOR DRYING Spring.
DRYING METHODS Press individual flowers in flower press or dry in desiccant.

Freesia
One of the most fragrant cut flowers. The stems of waxy flowers open one or two at a time and are available in a wide variety of colors. They last well in water.
AVAILABILITY Summer. All year from florists.

CONDITIONING (FRESH) Stand in deep water for several hours.
PICKING FOR DRYING Summer.
DRYING METHODS Dry with desiccant or press in flower press.

Fritillaria
A large genus of bulbous plants, the most common of which is the snake's-head fritillary with its solitary, nodding purple or white checkered bells. Crown imperials are much larger with a cluster of yellow or orange-red bells on the top of the stem, and leaves that look like a pineapple. Not suitable for drying.
AVAILABILITY Spring.
CONDITIONING (FRESH) Stand in deep water for several hours.

Fuchsia
Small shrubs with pendulous flowers, usually bell-shaped, in a range of pinks, purples and reds. Some forms have variegated foliage. Only a few are hardy.
AVAILABILITY Summer, autumn.
CONDITIONING (FRESH) Scrape, slit and recut stems and then stand in deep water for several hours.
PICKING FOR DRYING Summer and autumn.
DRYING METHODS Press flowers in flower press or dry in desiccant.

Gaillardia **Blanket flower**
Bright daisylike flowers in glowing shades of red, yellow and orange in summer. There are double and single forms. Last well in water.
AVAILABILITY Summer, autumn.
CONDITIONING (FRESH) Stand in deep water for several hours.
PICKING FOR DRYING Summer and autumn.
DRYING METHODS Press flowers in flower press.

Garrya **Silk tassel bush**
Valuable evergreen shrubs that have flowers in the form of long, silky, green tassels throughout

the winter at a time when there is not much else around. Last well in water.
AVAILABILITY Winter.
CONDITIONING (FRESH) Scrape, slit and recut stems and then stand in deep water for several hours.
PICKING FOR DRYING Winter.
DRYING METHODS Preserve by standing in glycerine when tassels mature.

Genista **Broom**
Arching branches of yellow pea-shaped flowers. Some fragrant species. Last quite well in water.
AVAILABILITY Early summer.
CONDITIONING (FRESH) Slit and recut stems and then stand in deep water for several hours.
PICKING FOR DRYING Summer.
DRYING METHODS Stems (after flowers dead): air dry by hanging or preserve by standing in glycerine. Flowers: dry in desiccant.

Gentiana **Gentian**
Upright trumpets of bright blue. The majority are short-stemmed but there are some bigger subjects, such as *G. asclepiadea*, which is up to 2 feet tall. Some species have white varieties.
AVAILABILITY Spring to late autumn.
CONDITIONING (FRESH) Stand in water in a warm, light place to open fully.
PICKING FOR DRYING Autumn.
DRYING METHODS Dry with desiccant.

Geranium **Crane's bill**
Popular herbaceous perennials with saucer-shaped flowers. There is a vast number of species available in colors ranging from the basic blue, mauve and purple, to red, pink and white, many having contrasting veining. Vary in height from small to tall. Not long lasting. The seedheads are attractive.
AVAILABILITY Late spring to autumn.

CONDITIONING (FRESH) Stand in deep water for several hours.
PICKING FOR DRYING Late summer to autumn.
DRYING METHODS Press flowers and leaves in flower press.

Gerbera **Transvaal daisy**
Brightly colored, daisylike flowers in cream, yellow, orange, red, pink or purple. Half-hardy perennials. Last well in water. Not suitable for drying.
AVAILABILITY All year from florist.
CONDITIONING (FRESH) Dip stem ends in boiling water and then stand in deep water for several hours.

Geum
Herbaceous perennials with brilliant red, yellow or orange flowers. There are single, semi-double or double flowers, the general shape being circular. Tend to hang their heads.
AVAILABILITY Late spring and summer.
CONDITIONING (FRESH) Dip stem ends in boiling water and then stand in deep water for several hours.
PICKING FOR DRYING Late spring and summer.
DRYING METHODS Press single forms in flower press and dry semidouble and double forms in desiccant.

Gladiolus
These are well-known bulbous plants with tall, slightly arching stems of brightly colored flowers. The leaves are long and swordlike. Most colors are available except true blue. Last well in water.
AVAILABILITY Summer, autumn.
CONDITIONING (FRESH) Remove top buds, slit and recut stems and then stand in deep water for several hours.
PICKING FOR DRYING Summer and autumn.
DRYING METHODS Dry smaller flowers in desiccant.

Glaucium Horned-poppy
Bright yellow or orange-red, papery flowers set off against a grayish stem and foliage. Long curved seed pods whence comes its common name. Not suitable for drying.
AVAILABILITY Summer, autumn.
CONDITIONING (FRESH) Stand in deep water for several hours.

Gomphrena Globe amaranth
Of the many species *G. globosa* is the main one in cultivation. Annuals with globular flowers of white, yellow, orange, red, pink and purple. Flowers are "everlasting" and can be easily dried.
AVAILABILITY Summer.
CONDITIONING (FRESH) Stand in deep water for several hours.
PICKING FOR DRYING Summer.
DRYING METHODS Air dry by hanging.

Grevillea
Tender shrubs useful for their evergreen, fernlike foliage and petaless flowers in yellow and red. Last well when cut.
AVAILABILITY Summer.
CONDITIONING (FRESH) Scrape, slit and recut stems and then stand in deep water for several hours.
PICKING FOR DRYING Summer.
DRYING METHODS Air dry leaves by hanging or preserve by standing in glycerine.

Grimmia Bun moss
Brilliant green mounds of moss make an ideal base for dried-flower trees or for "landscape" arrangements or basket displays of bright spring flowers. Conditioning not necessary for fresh arrangements.
PICKING FOR DRYING Summer.
DRYING METHODS Air dry in basket or box.

Griselinia
Evergreen shrubs which are valuable for their foliage, particularly in the variegated forms. All are long-lasting.

AVAILABILITY All year.
CONDITIONING (FRESH) Scrape, slit and recut stems and then stand in deep water for several hours.
PICKING FOR DRYING All year.
DRYING METHODS Preserve by standing in glycerine.

Gypsophila Baby's breath
Marvelous airy plants with fine wiry stems and little puffs of dainty white flowers. Pink varieties also available. Long lasting in water.
AVAILABILITY Summer.
CONDITIONING (FRESH) Stand in deep water for several hours.
PICKING FOR DRYING Summer.
DRYING METHODS Air dry by standing in container with a little water or hanging. Press flowers in flower press or dry in desiccant.

Hamamelis Witch hazel
Deciduous shrubs with flowers made up of clusters of spidery, straplike yellow petals on the naked branches. The flowers are fragrant. Autumn foliage is useful for pressed-flower pictures.
AVAILABILITY Late winter.
CONDITIONING (FRESH) Scrape, slit and recut stems then stand in deep water for several hours.
PICKING FOR DRYING Autumn.
DRYING METHODS Press individual leaves in flower press.

Hebe
A group of mainly New Zealand evergreen shrubs with dense spikes of blue, white or pink flowers. Some are scented. A few species are hardy; the rest need winter protection.
AVAILABILITY Summer, autumn.
CONDITIONING (FRESH) Scrape, slit and recut stems. Dip stem ends in boiling water and then stand in deep water for several hours.
PICKING FOR DRYING Summer and autumn.
DRYING METHODS Preserve leaves by standing in glycerine.

Hedera Ivy
Creeping foliage plants with distinctive leaves. There is considerable variation in size of leaf and the markings found on them. There are many variegated forms. Long-lasting. Also available as houseplants. Add a little green dye to glycerine when preserving to maintain color.
AVAILABILITY All year.
CONDITIONING (FRESH) Slit and recut stems and then stand in deep water for several hours. Dip ends of young stems in boiling water.
PICKING FOR DRYING All year.
DRYING METHODS Press in flower press or preserve by standing in glycerine.

Helenium Sneezeweed
Clusters of yellow, daisylike flowers on top of medium-length stems. Orange and brown varieties also available. Last quite well in water.
AVAILABILITY Summer, autumn.
CONDITIONING (FRESH) Slit and recut stems and then stand in deep water for several hours.
PICKING FOR DRYING Summer and autumn.
DRYING METHODS Dry flowers in desiccant.

Helianthus Sunflower
Very tall, yellow daisylike flowers. The well-known annual sunflower has a large, dark central disk. The perennial species are all much smaller.
AVAILABILITY Autumn.
CONDITIONING (FRESH) Dip stem ends in boiling water, then stand in deep water for several hours.
PICKING FOR DRYING Autumn.
DRYING METHODS Dry smaller flowers in desiccant.

Helichrysum
Everlastings, strawflowers
Very colorful daisylike flowers with papery bracts instead of petals. They can be yellow, brown, orange, red or pink in color. Fresh flowers last very well and are good dried.

AVAILABILITY Summer.
CONDITIONING (FRESH) Stand in deep water for several hours.
PICKING FOR DRYING Summer before fully open.
DRYING METHODS Air dry by hanging.

Helipterum
Acroclinium, rhodanthe

These delicate daisies are really fresh-looking when dried, especially when grouped in bunches in an arrangement. Extremely versatile flowers, they look good in large and small arrangements, by themselves or mixed with other dried flowers.
AVAILABILITY Summer.
CONDITIONING (FRESH) Stand in deep water for several hours.
PICKING FOR DRYING Summer before fully open.
DRYING METHODS Air dry by hanging.

Helleborus Christmas rose, Lenten rose, hellebore

An interesting range of saucer-shaped, winter flowers varying in color from the white Christmas rose through to the plum-colored and spotted Lenten roses. The green and stinking hellebores tend to have smaller, more cup-shaped flowers.
AVAILABILITY Winter, spring.
CONDITIONING (FRESH) Prick the stems with a pin. Dip stem ends in boiling water and then stand in deep water for several hours.
PICKING FOR DRYING Winter and spring.
DRYING METHODS Dry flowers in desiccant, preserve leaves by standing in glycerine. Press leaves and flowers in flower press.

Heracleum

Very tall plants with cartwheels of white flowers, like giant Queen Anne's lace. Sap can cause skin irritation. Seedheads can be used dried.
AVAILABILITY Late summer.

CONDITIONING (FRESH) Dip stem ends in boiling water and then stand in deep water for several hours.
PICKING FOR DRYING Autumn.
DRYING METHODS Air dry by standing in container with a little water or preserve by standing in glycerine.

Heuchera Coral bells

Sprays of airy flowers on thin stems. Colors include white, cream, pink and red. Last quite well in water.
AVAILABILITY Summer.
CONDITIONING (FRESH) Stand in deep water for several hours.
PICKING FOR DRYING Summer.
DRYING METHODS Press individual leaves and sprays in flower press or dry sprays in desiccant.

Hibiscus

Exotic trumpet-shaped flowers borne on tender shrubs and perennials. Each flower lasts only a day, and is then replaced by more. They are available in the full range of tropical colors. Not suitable for drying.
AVAILABILITY Late summer and autumn.
CONDITIONING (FRESH) Slit and recut stems, dip stem ends in boiling water and then stand in deep water for several hours.

Hippeastrum Amaryllis

Large lily-type flowers radiating from a tall stem. White, pink or red. Straplike leaves. Bulbous. Not suitable for drying.
AVAILABILITY Winter, spring.
CONDITIONING (FRESH) Fill hollow stem with water, plug end with cotton ball and stand in deep water for several hours. If head is heavy, support with wire pushed up hollow stem.

Hosta Plantain lily, funkia

Marvelous for both their foliage and spikes of flowers. The leaves are large and heart-shaped in varying shades of green and steely blue. There are also many

variegated forms. The flowers are either white, lilac-blue or purple. Long lasting in water.
AVAILABILITY Summer, autumn.
CONDITIONING (FRESH) Submerge leaves for a few minutes and then stand in water for several hours.
PICKING FOR DRYING Summer.
DRYING METHODS Dry flat or press between newspaper under carpet where there is no traffic or in flower press. Preserve foliage by immersing in glycerine.

Humulus Hops

Flowers have greenish bracts. Pick well before the heads ripen. Otherwise, they will fall apart as they dry. Hops tend to lose their color quickly once dry.
AVAILABILITY Flowers: summer.
CONDITIONING Slit and recut stems and then stand in deep water for several hours.
PICKING FOR DRYING Early autumn.
DRYING METHODS Air dry by hanging or preserve by standing in glycerine.

Hyacinthoides Scilla, bluebell

Arching stems of blue bells and straplike leaves. Pink and white varieties also available. Fragrant.
AVAILABILITY Spring.
CONDITIONING (FRESH) Stand in deep water for several hours.
PICKING FOR DRYING Spring.
DRYING METHODS Dry individual flowers in desiccant.

Hyacinthus Hyacinth

Bulbous plants with spikes of very fragrant flowers in blue, white and pink.
AVAILABILITY Spring. Winter if forced.
CONDITIONING (FRESH) Stand in deep water for several hours. Support stems with wires.
PICKING FOR DRYING Spring.
DRYING METHODS Dry individual flowers in desiccant.

Hydrangea

Shrubs with large rounded flowerheads. White, blue, mauve,

pink and red. There are also varieties with pointed spikes of flowers and delicate lacecaps, with just a few large, sterile florets round the edge of tiny, fertile florets.

AVAILABILITY Summer, autumn.
CONDITIONING (FRESH) Slit and recut stems and then stand in deep water for several hours.
PICKING FOR DRYING Autumn.
DRYING METHODS Air dry by hanging or by standing in container with a little water when bracts feel papery. Preserve leaves by standing in glycerine. Press individual bracts in flower press. Dried hydrangea flowerheads are very delicate.

Hypericum
Shrubs and subshrubs with saucer-shaped, golden-yellow flowers. Several good fruiting forms including *H. calycinum* (St John's wort).

AVAILABILITY Summer, autumn.
CONDITIONING (FRESH) Slit and recut stems and stand in deep water for several hours.
PICKING FOR DRYING Summer and autumn.
DRYING METHODS Press individual flowers in flower press.

Iberis **Candytuft**
Flat or domed heads of white flowers. Also pink and mauve varieties. Short-stemmed. Last very well in water. Seedheads can be dried on plant.

AVAILABILITY Spring.
CONDITIONING (FRESH) Stand in deep water for several hours.
PICKING FOR DRYING Summer
DRYING METHODS Preserve seedheads by standing in glycerine.

Ilex **Holly**
Glossy prickly-leaved shrubs or trees useful for their foliage and bright red berries borne in midwinter. There are variegated and yellow-berried forms. Flowers are insignificant, but leaves last well in water.

AVAILABILITY Winter.

CONDITIONING (FRESH) Scrape, slit and recut stems and then stand in deep water for several hours.
PICKING FOR DRYING Summer.
DRYING METHODS Preserve by standing in glycerine.

Iris **Flag**
Flowers that cover a long season starting with *I. unguicularis* in early winter, followed by the tiny reticulatas in winter and spring, and finally the taller species in summer. Some are scented. Not suitable for drying.

AVAILABILITY Winter, spring and summer. All year from florists.
CONDITIONING (FRESH) Stand in deep water for several hours.

Ixia
Slender-stemmed bulbous plants with several starlike flowers per stem. A large range of colours including bluish green. Last well in water. Tender.

AVAILABILITY Spring.
CONDITIONING (FRESH) Stand in deep water for several hours.
PICKING FOR DRYING Spring.
DRYING METHODS Press flowers in flower press.

Ixodia
The creamy-white heads of the little, waxy daisy flowers are extremely pretty and have a very fresh look when dried. They mix well in arrangements with all sorts of old-fashioned "country" or woodland flowers.

AVAILABILITY Summer.
CONDITIONING (FRESH) Stand in deep water for several hours.
PICKING FOR DRYING Summer.
DRYING METHODS Air dry by hanging.

Jasminum **Jasmine**
Both winter and summer forms. The former has starry yellow flowers on arching stems. In the summer there are white forms which are extremely fragrant. There are also yellow and pink forms available in summer.

AVAILABILITY Winter, summer.
CONDITIONING (FRESH) Stand in deep water for several hours immediately after cutting stems.
PICKING FOR DRYING Winter and summer.
DRYING METHODS Press individual flowers in flower press.

Juniperus **Juniper**
Columnar or spreading evergreen conifers giving all-year-round foliage. Color varies from green and blue to gold. The dwarf *J. communis* 'Compressa' is small enough for the whole tree to be used if potted.

AVAILABILITY All year.
CONDITIONING (FRESH) Scrape, slit and recut stems and then stand in deep water for several hours.
PICKING FOR DRYING Summer.
DRYING METHODS Dry separate cones in box.

Kalanchoe
Tender succulents usually grown as house plants that flower throughout the year. Flowers can be white, pink, red or yellow. Not suitable for drying.

AVAILABILITY All year.
CONDITIONING Stand flowers in deep water for several hours.

Kniphofia **Red-hot poker, torch lily**
Tall upright stems with a colorful spike of red, orange or yellow flowers. Not long lasting.

AVAILABILITY Summer, autumn.
CONDITIONING (FRESH) Stand in deep water for several hours.
PICKING FOR DRYING Summer and autumn.
DRYING METHODS Dry individual flowers in desiccant.

Kochia **Burning bush, summer cypress**
Fine-leaved plants that are said to resemble true cypress. They are bright-green turning dark-red in autumn.

AVAILABILITY Summer, autumn.
CONDITIONING (FRESH) Stand in

deep water for several hours.
PICKING FOR DRYING Summer and autumn.
DRYING METHODS Air dry by hanging.

Laburnum **Golden chain**
Trees with pendulous tassels of yellow pealike flowers. Seeds are very poisonous.
AVAILABILITY Early summer.
CONDITIONING (FRESH) Dip stem ends in boiling water and then stand in deep water for several hours.
PICKING FOR DRYING Summer.
DRYING METHODS Press individual flowers in flower press.

Lachenalia
Tender bulbous plants with a spike of numerous bell-shaped flowers in yellow, orange and red. Normally grown in greenhouse. Last well in water.
AVAILABILITY Winter and spring.
CONDITIONING (FRESH) Stand in deep water for several hours.
PICKING FOR DRYING Winter.
DRYING METHODS Press individual flowers in flower press or dry in desiccant.

Larix **Larch**
Deciduous conifers best in spring when the light-green, new growth is supplemented by the newly forming cones which are pink or red. Branches with sprays of small cones can be used in winter.
AVAILABILITY Foliage: spring. Cones: winter.
CONDITIONING (FRESH) Scrape, slit and recut stems and then stand in deep water for several hours. Dip ends of young stems in boiling water.
PICKING FOR DRYING Autumn.
DRYING METHODS Air dry branches by hanging and separate cones in basket.

Lathyrus **Sweet pea**
Sweet peas are justly well loved for their grace and fresh smell. There is now a vast range of cultivars from which to choose. Not all are fragrant. The long-stemmed flowers last quite well in water. There are also many other species which are perennial but these lack scent and also have a more restricted color range. Sweet peas are not suitable for drying.
AVAILABILITY Summer.
CONDITIONING (FRESH) Stand in deep water for several hours.

Lavandula **Lavender**
Gray-leaved shrubs with spikes of pale-purple flowers on long stems. The plants are very strongly scented. There are darker-purple and white forms. Pick flowers just as buds begin to open; any later and flowers will drop off. Drying them fast in a warm cupboard helps to fix the flowers.
AVAILABILITY Summer, autumn.
CONDITIONING (FRESH) Stand in deep water for several hours.
PICKING FOR DRYING Summer.
DRYING METHODS Air dry by hanging.

Lavatera **Tree mallow**
Annuals with bright-pink or white trumpets. Also perennial species but these are less interesting. Last reasonably well in water after cutting.
AVAILABILITY Summer, autumn.
CONDITIONING (FRESH) Dip stem ends in boiling water and then stand in deep water for several hours.
PICKING FOR DRYING Summer and autumn.
DRYING METHODS Press flowers in flower press or dry in desiccant.

Leptospermum
Popular New Zealand shrub in mild conditions. Branches are covered with masses of small white, pink or red flowers. Leaves are evergreen.
AVAILABILITY Summer.
CONDITIONING (FRESH) Scrape, slit and recut stems and then stand in deep water for several hours.
PICKING FOR DRYING Summer.
DRYING METHODS Air dry flower stems by standing in container in a little water.

Leucodendron **Protea, silver bush**
These woody seeding cones, often growing on stems with pale greenish silver leaves, are like flowers and have a strong form that looks very well in autumnal-colored arrangements.
AVAILABILITY Summer.
CONDITIONING (FRESH) Slit and recut stems and then stand in deep water for several hours.
PICKING FOR DRYING Summer.
DRYING METHODS Air dry hanging or standing in container without water.

Liatris **Gayfeather**
Several species of long, purple spikes of feathery flowers. Unusual in that they flower from tip of spike downward. For drying, pick when most of the flowers have opened. Last well in water.
AVAILABILITY Summer, autumn.
CONDITIONING (FRESH) Stand in deep water for several hours.
PICKING FOR DRYING Summer.
DRYING METHODS Air dry by hanging.

Ligustrum **Privet**
Evergreen shrubs useful for their foliage. Available in golden colors as well as green. White flowers with a scent that some find nasty, others attractive. Black berries in autumn.
AVAILABILITY All year.
CONDITIONING (FRESH) Slit and recut stems and then stand in deep water for several hours.
PICKING FOR DRYING Summer.
DRYING METHODS Preserve green form by standing in glycerine.

Lilium **Lily**
Beautiful, well-loved flowers shaped like either large trumpets

or turks' caps with curled back petals. Large range of colors (except blue), either plain or spotted. Many are fragrant. Last very well in water.
AVAILABILITY Summer and autumn. All year from florists.
CONDITIONING (FRESH) Stand in deep water for several hours.
PICKING FOR DRYING Summer and autumn.
DRYING METHODS Flowers: dry with desiccant or press in flower press. Seedheads: air dry by hanging.

Limonium **Sea lavender, statice**
Brightly colored flowers that last very well in water. A large range of colors is available, with blue, yellow and pink predominating.
AVAILABILITY Summer and autumn. All year from florists.
CONDITIONING (FRESH) Stand in deep water for several hours.
PICKING FOR DRYING Summer.
DRYING METHODS Air dry hanging or standing in container without water.

Lonicera **Honeysuckle**
Well-known and well-loved climbing plants which produce very heavily scented flowers, particularly strong in the evening. Various colors are available, including yellow, orange and red. There are also variegated-leaved forms. Do not last very long in water after cutting.
AVAILABILITY Summer, autumn.
CONDITIONING (FRESH) Stand in deep water for several hours.
PICKING FOR DRYING Summer and autumn.
DRYING METHODS Press flowers in flower press.

Lunaria **Honesty**
Biennial and perennial plants that do double service. In spring they have purple or white flowers. There are varieties with good variegated foliage. Later they have almost transparent, silky

seed-cases that are extremely useful in dried arrangements.
AVAILABILITY Flowers: spring. Seed-cases: autumn.
CONDITIONING (FRESH) Stand in deep water for several hours.
PICKING FOR DRYING Autumn.
DRYING METHODS Dry seed-cases on the plant and remove outer scales or air dry by hanging or standing in container with no water. Preserve green seed-cases by standing in glycerine.

Lupinus **Lupine**
Old-fashioned, cottage garden plants with spires of pealike flowers. Large number of cultivars available in a good range of colors including yellow, blue, white, pink and orange. Peppery scent. Last very well in water.
AVAILABILITY Summer.
CONDITIONING (FRESH) Fill hollow stems with water and plug with cotton ball, or dip stem ends in boiling water. Stand in deep water for several hours.
PICKING FOR DRYING Summer.
DRYING METHODS Dry individual flowers in desiccant or press in flower press.

Lysimachia **Loosestrife**
Spikes of bright-yellow, cup-shaped flowers. The spikes are clothed with whorls of flowers backed by leaves. Last quite well in water.
AVAILABILITY Summer.
CONDITIONING (FRESH) Stand in deep water for several hours.
PICKING FOR DRYING Summer.
DRYING METHODS Press individual flowers in flower press.

Lythrum **Purple loosestrife**
Tall herbaceous plants that have spires of brilliant-purple flowers. They do not last very long in water but add a good vertical emphasis, with a splash of strong color, to arrangements. Not suitable for drying.
AVAILABILITY Late summer and autumn.
CONDITIONING (FRESH) Dip stem

ends in boiling water and then stand in deep water for several hours.

Magnolia
Deciduous and evergreen shrubs and trees with predominantly white flowers, flushed sometimes with pink. Some varieties are scented.
AVAILABILITY Spring and summer.
CONDITIONING (FRESH) Scrape, slit and recut stems. Dip stem ends in boiling water and then stand in deep water for several hours.
PICKING FOR DRYING Spring and summer.
DRYING METHODS Leaves: preserve by standing in glycerine. Flowers: dry with desiccant.

Mahonia
Evergreen shrubs with glossy, spiny leaves and spikes of fragrant yellow flowers. Blue-black fruit in autumn.
AVAILABILITY Foliage: all year. Flowers: winter, spring. Fruit: autumn.
CONDITIONING (FRESH) Scrape, slit and recut stems and then stand in deep water for several hours.
PICKING FOR DRYING Summer.
DRYING METHODS Preserve by standing in glycerine.

Malus **Crab apple**
Deciduous trees with pink-tinged blossom in spring, and shiny green, yellow or red apples of various sizes in the autumn. Some have decorative foliage.
AVAILABILITY Blossom: spring. Foliage: summer, autumn. Fruit: autumn.
CONDITIONING (FRESH) Scrape, slit and recut stems and then stand in deep water for several hours.
PICKING FOR DRYING Spring and autumn.
DRYING METHODS Air dry fruits by standing branches in container in a little water. Press flowers in flower press.

Matteucia
Ostrich feather fern
The dried fronds of this beautiful fern, which grows like a shuttle-cock, can be used like fresh fern.
AVAILABILITY Summer.
CONDITIONING (FRESH) Dip ends of young stems in boiling water and stand in deep water for several hours.
PICKING FOR DRYING Summer.
DRYING METHODS Air dry flat or press between newspaper under carpet where there is no traffic.

Matthiola Stock
Annuals and biennials, which are among the most popular cut flowers, with small-spired, soft-colored, scented flowers. Good range of pink, purple, white, yellow and cream. Last quite well in water.
AVAILABILITY Summer. Florists: spring and summer.
CONDITIONING (FRESH) Stand in deep water for several hours.
PICKING FOR DRYING Summer.
DRYING METHODS Dry individual flowers in desiccant.

Miscanthus
Tall ornamental grasses valuable for their foliage and plumed seed-heads. Several variegated forms including one with horizontal yellow stripes on the leaves. The blue-green leaves and fronds dry to a beige color.
AVAILABILITY Summer.
CONDITIONING (FRESH) Stand in deep water for several hours.
PICKING FOR DRYING Summer and autumn.
DRYING METHODS Air dry by hanging or by standing in container without water.

Moluccella Bells of Ireland, shell flower
Tall stems of green trumpets in which sit tiny white flowers. The green calyces continue long after the flower dies. Last very well in water. For drying, they should be picked just as the first flowers emerge.

AVAILABILITY Summer, autumn.
CONDITIONING (FRESH) Remove all leaves, dip stem ends in boiling water and then stand in deep water for several hours.
PICKING FOR DRYING Summer.
DRYING METHODS Remove all leaves and air dry by hanging or preserve by standing in glycerine.

Monarda Bergamot, bee balm
Whorls of red, pink or white flowers that seem to spring from a pincushion at the top of the stem. Very aromatic foliage.
AVAILABILITY Summer, autumn.
CONDITIONING (FRESH) Stand in deep water for several hours.
PICKING FOR DRYING Summer and autumn.
DRYING METHODS Air dry flowers by hanging.

Muscari Grape hyacinth
Small-stemmed bulbs with spikes of varying shades of blue or white scented flowers.
AVAILABILITY Spring.
CONDITIONING (FRESH) Stand in deep water for several hours.
PICKING FOR DRYING Spring.
DRYING METHODS Dry flowers in desiccant.

Myosotis Forget-me-not
Short arching sprays of blue flowers. Last quite well in water.
AVAILABILITY Late spring and summer.
CONDITIONING (FRESH) Stand in deep water for several hours. Keep cool.
PICKING FOR DRYING Spring and summer.
DRYING METHODS Press in flower press.

Narcissus Daffodil, jonquil
Very popular spring bulbs with trumpets or cups coming from a disk of petals. Mainly yellow but white, orange and pink varieties are also available. In addition, there are many forms of minia-ture daffodil including the jonquils. Many are fragrant.

AVAILABILITY Spring. Florists: winter and spring.
CONDITIONING (FRESH) Cut in bud. Stand in deep water for several hours.
PICKING FOR DRYING Spring.
DRYING METHODS Dry with desiccant, crystallize or press in flower press.

Nepeta Catmint
Airy stems of pale-blue or mauve flowers set off against gray foliage. The foliage is fragrant, particularly when crushed. Last quite well in water.
AVAILABILITY Summer.
CONDITIONING (FRESH) Stand in deep water for several hours.
PICKING FOR DRYING Summer.
DRYING METHODS Air dry by hanging.

Nephrolepis Ladder, fishbone or sword fern
Evergreen ferns that are usually grown as pot plants. The cut fronds last well in water and can be pressed successfully.
AVAILABILITY All year.
CONDITIONING (FRESH) Stand in deep water for several hours.
PICKING FOR DRYING All year.
DRYING METHODS Press between newspaper under carpet where there is no traffic.

Nerine
Autumnal bulbous plants with clusters of pink trumpetlike flowers, which are very long-lasting in water.
AVAILABILITY Autumn.
CONDITIONING (FRESH) Stand in deep water for several hours.
PICKING FOR DRYING Autumn.
DRYING METHODS Dry individual flowers in desiccant.

Nicotiana Flowering tobacco
Annual starry-flowered plants coming in a variety of colors, the greens being particularly important. Some varieties very fragrant, particularly after dark. Last well in water.
AVAILABILITY Summer, autumn.

CONDITIONING (FRESH) Stand in deep water for several hours.
PICKING FOR DRYING Summer and autumn.
DRYING METHODS Dry flowers in desiccant or press in flower press.

Nigella Love-in-a-mist
Hardy annuals with blue flowers and a collar of bright-green, feathery foliage. Last very well in water. The almost spherical seedheads are very beautiful and dry easily. The flowers need to be placed in a warm cupboard or warming oven for best results.
AVAILABILITY Summer.
CONDITIONING (FRESH) Stand in deep water for several hours.
PICKING FOR DRYING Summer, early autumn.
DRYING METHODS Air dry seedheads by hanging.

Ornithogalum Star of Bethlehem, Chincherinchee
Bulbs with either sprays or spikes of small white flowers. Last very well in water.
AVAILABILITY Spring. All year from florists.
CONDITIONING (FRESH) Stand in deep water for several hours.
PICKING FOR DRYING Spring.
DRYING METHODS Dry individual flowers in desiccant or press in flower press.

Osmunda
Tall deciduous varieties of fern.
AVAILABILITY Summer.
CONDITIONING (FRESH) Stand in deep water for several hours. Dip ends of young stems in boiling water.
PICKING FOR DRYING Summer.
DRYING METHODS Air dry flat or press between newpaper under carpet where there is no traffiic.

Paeonia Peony
Herbaceous or shrubby plants. Large bold flowerheads of red, white, yellow or pink. Can be single or double. Some varieties are also scented.
AVAILABILITY Summer.
CONDITIONING (FRESH) Dip stem ends in boiling water and then stand in deep water for several hours.
PICKING FOR DRYING Summer.
DRYING METHODS Dry with desiccant, air dry by hanging or press petals in flower press.

Papaver Poppy
Brightly colored flowers with tissuelike petals. Not long lasting in water: pick when bud showing color.
AVAILABILITY Summer, autumn.
CONDITIONING (FRESH) Cut as buds open. Seal sappy stem over small flame or dip in boiling water and then stand in deep water for several hours.
PICKING FOR DRYING Summer.
DRYING METHODS Air dry seedheads by hanging or preserve by standing in glycerine. Press flowers in flower press.

Pelargonium Geranium
Tender plants with very colorful heads of flowers in bright reds, pinks, purples and white. Some leaves are fragrant and others have good zonal markings.
AVAILABILITY Summer, autumn.
CONDITIONING (FRESH) Stand in deep water for several hours.
PICKING FOR DRYING Summer and autumn.
DRYING METHODS Press leaves and individual flowers in flower press.

Penstemon
Spikes of tubular flowers of bright or more subtle colors. Available in a range of red, pink, purple and blue. Do not last long in water.
AVAILABILITY Summer, autumn.
CONDITIONING (FRESH) Stand in deep water for several hours.
PICKING FOR DRYING Summer and autumn.
DRYING METHODS Press individual flowers in flower press or dry in desiccant.

Pernettya
Low shrubs with small bell-shaped flowers, but it is the mass of round berries which clothe the stems that are most useful in arrangements. Available in a range of colors: white, pink and red. Evergreen.
AVAILABILITY Flowers: summer. Berries: autumn.
CONDITIONING (FRESH) Scrape, slit and recut stems and then stand in deep water for several hours.
PICKING FOR DRYING Summer.
DRYING METHODS Dry sprays of flowers in desiccant.

Peucedanum
Flat heads of white, yellow or pink flowers.
AVAILABILITY Summer.
CONDITIONING (FRESH) Stand in deep water for several hours.
PICKING FOR DRYING Summer.
DRYING METHODS Air dry by hanging or preserve seedheads by standing in glycerine.

Phaenocoma
Phaenocoma shrub
The flowers are a particularly vivid pink, stronger than both helipterum and helichrysum, both of which they resemble. They are set off by the tiny silver-gray leaves.
AVAILABILITY Summer.
CONDITIONING (FRESH) Stand in deep water for several hours.
PICKING FOR DRYING Summer.
DRYING METHODS Air dry by hanging.

Phaseolus Bean
Climbing plants with white, red, purple or yellow, pealike flowers. Not suitable for drying.
AVAILABILITY Summer, autumn.
CONDITIONING (FRESH) Stand in deep water for several hours.

Philadelphus Mock orange
Hardy shrubs with heavily scented white flowers. There are double-flowered and golden-leaved forms.

AVAILABILITY Summer.
CONDITIONING (FRESH) Remove most of the leaves. Scrape, slit and recut stems. Dip stem ends in boiling water and then stand in deep water for several hours.
PICKING FOR DRYING Summer.
DRYING METHODS Press individual flowers in flower press or dry in desiccant.

Phlomis **Jerusalem sage**
Whorls of yellow sagelike flowers with soft felty leaves. Leaves do not last very well. Pick just as the yellow flowers start to open.
AVAILABILITY Summer.
CONDITIONING (FRESH) Slit and recut stems and then stand in deep water for several hours.
PICKING FOR DRYING Summer.
DRYING METHODS Air dry by hanging.

Phlox
Tall border plants with large heads of brightly colored flowers in white, blue, pink, red and mauve. Last well.
AVAILABILITY Summer.
CONDITIONING (FRESH) Slit and recut stems and then stand in deep water for several hours.
PICKING FOR DRYING Summer.
DRYING METHODS Press individual flowers in flower press.

Physalis **Chinese lantern, ground cherry**
Bright-orange paper lanterns enclosing the fruit make these plants decorative.
AVAILABILITY Autumn.
CONDITIONING (FRESH) Pick when orange begins to show. Remove leaves. Stand in deep water for several hours.
PICKING FOR DRYING Autumn.
DRYING METHODS Air dry by hanging.

Picea **Spruce**
Evergreen conifers used for their foliage, particularly as Christmas trees.

AVAILABILITY All year.
CONDITIONING (FRESH) Scrape, slit and recut stems and then stand in deep water for several hours.
PICKING FOR DRYING All year.
DRYING METHODS Air dry foliage in arrangements and separate cones in basket.

Pieris **Andromeda**
Evergreen shrubs with masses of lily-of-the-valley flowers hanging in bunches. The shiny young foliage is red in spring. Not suitable for drying.
AVAILABILITY Spring.
CONDITIONING (FRESH) Scrape, slit and recut stems and then stand in deep water for several hours. Dip ends of young stems in boiling water.

Pinus **Pine**
Evergreen conifers with needle-like leaves in bunches and cones. Good for winter arrangements.
AVAILABILITY All year.
CONDITIONING (FRESH) Scrape, slit and recut stems and then stand in deep water for several hours.
PICKING FOR DRYING Any time.
DRYING METHODS Air dry foliage in arrangements and separate cones in basket.

Pithocarpa **Miniature daisy**
These little white daisies are almost as delicate as gypsophila, but each flower has a more marked daisy shape. Very pretty and ideal for fresh, frothy arrangements.
AVAILABILITY Summer.
CONDITIONING (FRESH) Stand in deep water for several hours.
PICKING FOR DRYING Summer.
DRYING METHODS Air dry by hanging.

Pittosporum
Evergreen shrubs with useful shiny foliage. There are variegated and purple forms. Last well in water.
AVAILABILITY All year.

CONDITIONING (FRESH) Scrape, slit and recut stems and then stand in water for several hours.
PICKING FOR DRYING All year.
DRYING METHODS Preserve by standing in glycerine.

Platycodon **Balloon flower**
Called balloon flowers because of their interesting shape while in bud, when the flowers resemble inflated balloons. The flower itself is like a large open campanula in a rich blue. There are also white forms.
AVAILABILITY Summer.
CONDITIONING (FRESH) Dip stem ends in boiling water and then stand in deep water for several hours.
PICKING FOR DRYING Summer.
DRYING METHODS Press open flowers in flower press or dry in desiccant.

Polemonium **Jacob's ladder**
Spikes of white or blue, saucer-shaped flowers.
AVAILABILITY Late spring and summer.
CONDITIONING (FRESH) Stand in deep water for several hours.
PICKING FOR DRYING Spring and summer.
DRYING METHODS Press flowers and leaves in flower press.

Polianthes **Tuberose**
White-flowered, bulbous plants with very strong scent.
AVAILABILITY Summer. All year from florists.
CONDITIONING (FRESH) Stand in deep water for several hours.
PICKING FOR DRYING Summer.
DRYING METHODS Dry individual flowers in desiccant.

Polygonatum **Solomon's seal**
Graceful arching stems with small white bells hanging below the outstretched leaves. Very cool appearance.
AVAILABILITY Spring and early summer.
CONDITIONING (FRESH) Stand in deep water for several hours.

PICKING FOR DRYING Spring.
DRYING METHODS Dry with desiccant, or preserve by standing in glycerine.

Polygonum **Knotweed snakeweed**
Small or medium stems of pink or red flowers. Still look good when they have turned brown. Last well in water.
AVAILABILITY Summer, autumn.
CONDITIONING (FRESH) Dip stem ends in boiling water and then stand in deep water for several hours.
PICKING FOR DRYING Autumn.
DRYING METHODS Dry on plant.

Polystichum **Shield fern**
This evergreen fern is very finely divided and looks almost feather-like. The fronds are very attractive and look good when they are set among any other dried flowers.
AVAILABILITY Summer.
CONDITIONING (FRESH) Dip stem ends in boiling water and then stand in deep water for several hours.
PICKING FOR DRYING Summer.
DRYING METHODS Press between newspaper.

Populus **Poplar**
Deciduous trees or shrubs with shiny heart-shaped leaves. Silver and gold forms available. Flowers of no importance. Not suitable for drying.
AVAILABILITY Summer.
CONDITIONING (FRESH) Scrape, slit and recut stems and then stand in deep water for several hours. Dip ends of young stems in boiling water.

Primula **Cowslip, polyanthus, primrose**
Short-stemmed flowers, the majority of which are yellow, but other bright colors, including blue and mauve, are available. Many varieties are fragrant.
AVAILABILITY Spring. Winter as pot plants.

CONDITIONING (FRESH) Stand in deep water for several hours.
PICKING FOR DRYING Spring.
DRYING METHODS Dry with desiccant, press in flower press or crystallize.

Protea
Tender shrubs with large flower-heads of differing shapes in red, pink, white, yellow, orange and purple. They last a very long time in water. For drying, pick just as the bud begins to open; a rubber band will prevent the flower from opening too much.
AVAILABILITY All year round from florists.
CONDITIONING (FRESH) Scrape, slit and recut stems and then stand in deep water for several hours.
PICKING FOR DRYING Summer.
DRYING METHODS Air dry by hanging.

Prunus **Almond, cherry, nectarine, peach, plum**
Trees or shrubs bearing pink or white blossom. Many varieties have double flowers. Some flower very early. Last a few days in water.
AVAILABILITY Mainly spring, but also winter.
CONDITIONING (FRESH) Scrape, slit and recut stems. Dip ends of young stems in boiling water, and then stand in deep water for several hours.
PICKING FOR DRYING Spring.
DRYING METHODS Crystallize, press in flower press or dry in desiccant.

Pulmonaria **Lungwort**
Blue, purple, pink or red flowers on low-growing border plant. Some varieties have silver, variegated or spotted leaves.
AVAILABILITY Spring, but also some in winter.
CONDITIONING (FRESH) Stand in deep water for several hours.
PICKING FOR DRYING Spring.
DRYING METHODS Press flowers in flower press or crystallize.

Punica **Pomegranate**
A spherical fruit with a yellowish-red or brown skin.
AVAILABILITY Autumn from produce markets.

Pyrethrum
Daisylike flowers in bright colors: red, pink, and white. Feathery foliage. Last quite well in water.
AVAILABILITY Summer, autumn.
CONDITIONING (FRESH) Stand in deep water for several hours.
PICKING FOR DRYING Summer and autumn.
DRYING METHODS Press in flower press or dry in desiccant.

Pyrus **Pear**
Trees with attractive white blossom in spring, and yellow or green fruit in autumn. Not suitable for drying.
AVAILABILITY Blossom: spring. Fruit: autumn. All year from produce markets.
CONDITIONING (FRESH) Scrape, slit and recut stems and then stand in deep water for several hours. Home-grown fruit lasts longer.

Quercus **Oak**
All oak leaves press well, either in summer when they are green or in the autumn, as they begin to change color.
AVAILABILITY Spring to autumn.
CONDITIONING (FRESH) Scrape, slit and recut stems and then stand in deep water for several hours.
PICKING FOR DRYING Summer.
DRYING METHODS Press between newspaper under carpet where there is no traffic.

Ranunculus **Buttercup**
Apart from the native yellow varieties, there are many other larger, brightly colored forms with double flowers.
AVAILABILITY Summer. Florists: most of the year.
CONDITIONING (FRESH) Stand in deep water for several hours.

PICKING FOR DRYING Early summer.
DRYING METHODS Dry with desiccant or air dry by hanging. Press single varieties in flower press.

Rheum Rhubarb
The young leaves of the culinary and ornamental rhubarbs can be used. The leaves are poisonous. Not suitable for drying.
AVAILABILITY Spring.
CONDITIONING (FRESH) Submerge whole leaf for a short time and then stand in deep water for several hours.

Rhododendron
A very large family of evergreen shrubs with attractive clusters of yellow, white, pink, red and purple flowers.
AVAILABILITY Winter to autumn.
CONDITIONING (FRESH) Scrape, slit and recut stems and then stand in deep water for several hours.
PICKING FOR DRYING Leaves: all year. Flowers: spring and summer.
DRYING METHODS Leaves: preserve leaves by standing in glycerine. Flowers: press individual flowers in flower press or dry in desiccant.

Ribes Currant
Deciduous shrubs with hanging clusters of small, pink or red flowers and fresh, heavily veined leaves. Can be forced.
AVAILABILITY Spring.
CONDITIONING (FRESH) Scrape, slit and recut stems. Dip ends of young stems in boiling water, and then stand in deep water for several hours.
PICKING FOR DRYING Spring.
DRYING METHODS Press leaves in flower press.

Rosa Rose
A very large family of shrubs and climbers with a good range of colors. Many are fragrant and the majority have thorny stems.

The wonderfully fragrant hybrid tea roses air dry well when hung in a cool, dry, dark place. Single roses and double, old-fashioned roses must be dried with desiccants for best results. Pick all roses for drying before they are fully open.
AVAILABILITY Summer and autumn. Florists: all year.
CONDITIONING (FRESH) Best cut in bud when showing color. Remove thorns and then stand in deep water for several hours.
PICKING FOR DRYING Summer.
DRYING METHODS Air dry by hanging, dry with desiccant or press petals in flower press.

Rosmarinus Rosemary
Evergreen shrubs with small needlelike, gray leaves which are fragrant when crushed. Pale-blue flowers.
AVAILABILITY Foliage: all year. Flowers: summer and autumn.
CONDITIONING (FRESH) Slit and recut stems and then stand in deep water for several hours.
PICKING FOR DRYING All year.
DRYING METHODS Air dry by hanging or preserve by standing in glycerine.

Rubus Blackberry, Raspberry
Thorny rambling shrubs with mauve flowers and black berries, often both at the same time. Not suitable for drying.
AVAILABILITY Autumn.
CONDITIONING (FRESH) Scrape, slit and recut stems and then stand in deep water for several hours.

Rudbeckia Coneflower, black-eyed Susan
Bright yellow, orange and brown daisylike flowers with long rough stems. Single or double. Last well in water. Not suitable for drying.
AVAILABILITY Late summer and autumn.
CONDITIONING (FRESH) Dip stem ends in boiling water and then stand in deep water for several hours.

Ruscus Butcher's broom, box holly
Curious shrubs with modified stems that look like sharp-pointed leaves, the center of which carry bright red berries after insignificant flowers.
AVAILABILITY Foliage: all year. Berries: autumn.
CONDITIONING (FRESH) Scrape, slit and recut stems and then stand in deep water for several hours.
PICKING FOR DRYING All year.
DRYING METHODS Air dry leaves by hanging or preserve by standing in glycerine.

Ruta Rue
Shrubby herbs with deeply cut, blue-gray leaves which are very aromatic. The flowers are yellow but not frequently used.
AVAILABILITY Summer, autumn.
CONDITIONING (FRESH) Slit and recut stems and then stand in deep water for several hours.
PICKING FOR DRYING All year.
DRYING METHODS Press leaves in flower press.

Saintpaulia African violet
Very popular houseplants with dark-green, furry leaves and blue or purple flowers on short stems. Last quite well in water.
AVAILABILITY All year.
CONDITIONING (FRESH) Stand in deep water for several hours.
PICKING FOR DRYING All year.
DRYING METHODS Press individual flowers in flower press.

Salix Willow, pussy willow
Trees and shrubs with variation in bark color, which is useful during winter. The majority also bear interesting catkins which should be preserved before the yellow pollen appears.
AVAILABILITY Stems: winter. Catkins: late winter and spring. Foliage: spring to autumn.
CONDITIONING (FRESH) Scrape, slit and recut stems and then stand in deep water for several hours.

PICKING FOR DRYING All year.
DRYING METHODS Air dry foliage by hanging and preserve catkins by standing in glycerine.

Salvia Sage family

Shrubs and herbaceous perennials with long spikes of blue or purple flowers. Foliage often aromatic. Last quite well in water. The cottage variety 'Clary' dries well. *S farinacea* looks like rich colored lavender when dried.
AVAILABILITY Summer, autumn.
CONDITIONING (FRESH) Stand in deep water for several hours.
PICKING FOR DRYING Summer.
DRYING METHODS Air dry by hanging.

Sambucus Elder

Deciduous shrubs with large flat-headed clusters of white flowers. Many have interesting foliage, which can be purple, golden or variegated. Some have very finely cut leaves.
AVAILABILITY Flowers: spring. Foliage: spring to autumn. Berries: autumn.
CONDITIONING (FRESH) Scrape, slit and recut stems. Dip ends of young stems in boiling water, and then stand in deep water for several hours.
PICKING FOR DRYING Summer.
DRYING METHODS Press leaves in flower press or under carpet between newspaper where there is no traffic.

Santolina

Small evergreen shrubs with aromatic green or gray stems and foliage. Summer flowers are yellow but of little consequence. *S. neopolitana* is particularly good for drying.
AVAILABILITY All year.
CONDITIONING (FRESH) Scrape, slit and recut stems and then stand in deep water for several hours.
PICKING FOR DRYING Summer.
DRYING METHODS Air dry by hanging.

Scabiosa Scabious, pincushion flower

Blue, mauve, white or pale yellow disk-shaped flowers. There are double varieties available. Last quite well in water. The flowers shrink substantially when dried.
AVAILABILITY Summer.
CONDITIONING (FRESH) Stand in deep water for several hours.
PICKING FOR DRYING Summer and autumn.
DRYING METHODS Air dry by hanging or dry small mature flowers in desiccant.

Scilla Squill

Short-stemmed bulbs available with star- or bell-like flowers in blue, violet or white.
AVAILABILITY Spring.
CONDITIONING (FRESH) Stand in deep water for several hours.
PICKING FOR DRYING Spring.
DRYING METHODS Dry with desiccant or crystallize.

Sedum Stonecrop

Fleshy succulent plants with flat heads of red, pink or mauve. Smaller varieties are available with white or yellow flowers. Not suitable for drying.
AVAILABILITY Autumn.
CONDITIONING (FRESH) Stand in deep water for several hours.

Selaginella Club moss

This is a plant that looks good preserved in a glycerine solution to which green dye has been added to keep its natural, bright green colour. Club moss can be used as a base for arrangements or bunches can be used like foliage. Conditioning not necessary for fresh arrangements.
PICKING FOR DRYING All year.
DRYING METHODS Air dry in basket or box, or preserve in glycerine.

Senecio Ragwort, cineraria

Yellow daisylike flowers with valuable green or gray foliage *S. greyi* should be picked for drying well before the yellow flowers open, as it is the leaves and buds that are attractive when dried.
AVAILABILITY Summer.
CONDITIONING (FRESH) Slit and recut stems and then stand in deep water for several hours.
PICKING FOR DRYING Summer.
DRYING METHODS Air dry by hanging, or press individual leaves in flower press.

Silene Campion, catchfly

The delicate little pale-pink flowers of this garden campion look very fresh when dried.
AVAILABILITY Summer.
CONDITIONING (FRESH) Stand in deep water for several hours.
PICKING FOR DRYING Summer.
DRYING METHODS Air dry by hanging or press flowers in flower press.

Skimmia

Evergreen shrubs with glossy leaves and clusters of long-lasting red berries. White, scented flowers. Last well in water. Not suitable for drying.
AVAILABILITY Foliage: all year. Flowers: spring. Berries: autumn to spring.
CONDITIONING (FRESH) Scrape, slit and recut stems and then stand in deep water for several hours.

Solidago Goldenrod

Long-stemmed plants with fluffy, feathery yellow plumes. Last quite well in water. They can be dried well before the flowers open to use green or when flowers mature.
AVAILABILITY Summer, autumn.
CONDITIONING (FRESH) Stand in deep water for several hours.
PICKING FOR DRYING Summer to autumn.
DRYING METHODS Air dry by hanging.

Sorbus Mountain ash, rowan

Deciduous trees which are useful for the clusters of white flowers,

silvery foliage which has good autumn tints and orange, pink or white berries.
AVAILABILITY Flowers: spring. Foliage: summer or autumn. Berries: autumn.
CONDITIONING (FRESH) Scrape, slit and recut stems and then stand in deep water for several hours.
PICKING FOR DRYING Summer and autumn.
DRYING METHODS Press individual leaves in flower press.

Sphagnum **Sphagnum moss**
Invaluable as a base for many types of arrangement. Conditioning not necessary for fresh arrangements.
PICKING FOR DRYING Any time. Available from florists.
DRYING METHODS Air dry in basket or box.

Spiraea
Deciduous shrubs with masses of small white or pink flowers either in sprays or flat heads. There are variegated-leaved forms.
AVAILABILITY Spring.
CONDITIONING (FRESH) Scrape, slit and recut stems and then stand in deep water for several hours.
PICKING FOR DRYING Spring.
DRYING METHODS Dry flowers in desiccant.

Stachys **Lamb's ears**
Herbaceous plants with soft, felty gray or silver leaves and pale-pink flowers borne on tallish gray stems.
AVAILABILITY Summer, autumn.
CONDITIONING (FRESH) Stand in deep water for several hours, being careful not to wet foliage.
PICKING FOR DRYING Summer.
DRYING METHODS Leaves: air dry by hanging. Seedheads: preserve by standing in glycerine.

Staphylea
Deciduous shrubs with clusters of white, scented flowers in summer followed by curious,

translucent seed capsules which seem to be inflated. Not suitable for drying.
AVAILABILITY Flowers: summer. Seed capsules: autumn.
CONDITIONING (FRESH) Scrape, slit and recut stems and then stand in deep water for several hours.

Stranvaesia
Semideciduous shrubs whose red leaves when they are about to fall contrast well with the green ones staying on the plant. This contrast is also helped by clusters of red berries. None is suitable for drying.
AVAILABILITY Autumn.
CONDITIONING (FRESH) Scrape, slit and recut stems and then stand in deep water for several hours.

Strelitzia
Bird of paradise flower
Tropical brightly colored plants whose flower resembles the head of a bird with a bright, long-lasting orange crest. Not suitable for drying.
AVAILABILITY Spring. All year from florists.
CONDITIONING (FRESH) Stand in deep water for several hours.

Symphoricarpos **Snowberry**
Deciduous shrubs with insignificant pink flowers that produce white berries, which stay on the long naked stems. Not suitable for drying.
AVAILABILITY Autumn and winter.
CONDITIONING (FRESH) Scrape, slit and recut stems and then stand in deep water for several hours.

Syringa **Lilac**
Deciduous shrubs with large spikes of fragrant flowers in white and varying shades of mauve and purple.
AVAILABILITY Spring.
CONDITIONING (FRESH) Remove all leaves. Scrape, slit and recut stems. Dip stem ends in boiling

water and then stand in deep water for several hours.
PICKING FOR DRYING Spring.
DRYING METHODS Divide flowerheads into small sections and dry in desiccant.

Taxus **Yew**
Evergreen conifers with dark-green, narrow leaves. Also attractive, sticky red fruit in autumn. Some think it unlucky if brought into the house. Lasts very well in water. Yew dries well without dropping and it can be used as foliage in all-year-round displays.
AVAILABILITY Foliage: all year.
CONDITIONING (FRESH) Scrape, slit and recut stems and then stand in water for several hours.
PICKING FOR DRYING All year.
DRYING METHODS As for fresh and then dry in arrangement or air dry by hanging or standing in container with a little water.

Thalictrum **Meadow rue**
Tall plants with sprays of fluffy, yellow, mauve or purple flowers. The delicate foliage is finely cut and can be green, gray-green or blue-green.
AVAILABILITY Summer.
CONDITIONING (FRESH) Dip stem ends in boiling water if wilting and then stand in deep water for several hours.
PICKING FOR DRYING Summer.
DRYING METHODS Air dry by hanging, press flowers and leaves in flower press or dry flowers in desiccant.

Thymus **Thyme**
Dwarf shrubby herbs some of which are very fragrant, particularly if crushed. Pink, white, crimson, mauve or purple flowers on short stems.
AVAILABILITY Summer.
CONDITIONING (FRESH) Stand in deep water for several hours.
PICKING FOR DRYING Summer.
DRYING METHODS Air dry by hanging.

Tilia **Linden**

The color of the seed sprays can be enhanced by adding rust-colored dye to the glycerine solution to lend autumnal tints to the material.

AVAILABILITY Spring.

CONDITIONING (FRESH) Dip stem ends in boiling water and then stand in deep water for several hours.

PICKING FOR DRYING Summer.

DRYING METHODS Air dry by hanging, or preserve seed-sprays by standing in glycerine.

Tillandsia

One species, Spanish moss, looks like narrow gray hay. It makes a lacelike border for nosegays and ropes and can also be used to make wreaths. Not suitable for fresh arrangements.

PICKING FOR DRYING Any time.

DRYING METHODS Air dry.

Tricyrtis **Toad lily**

Sprays of intriguing white, mauve or yellow flowers, with heavy purple spotting, on tall arching stems. Last well in water. Not suitable for drying.

AVAILABILITY Autumn.

CONDITIONING (FRESH) Stand in deep water for several hours.

Trollius **Globe flower**

Yellow or orange flower like a large, double buttercup.

AVAILABILITY Late spring and early summer.

CONDITIONING (FRESH) Dip stem ends in boiling water and then stand in water for several hours.

PICKING FOR DRYING Autumn.

DRYING METHODS Press leaves in flower press and dry flowers in desiccant.

Tropaeolum **Nasturtium**

Floriferous annual available in a rainbow palette. Climbing and dwarf varieties are available. Last well in water.

AVAILABILITY Summer, autumn.

CONDITIONING (FRESH) Stand in deep water for several hours.

PICKING FOR DRYING Summer and autumn.

DRYING METHODS Press individual leaves and flowers in flower press.

Tulipa **Tulip**

Familiar bulbous plants with brightly colored chalices in a wide range of colors including near-black. Long lasting in water.

AVAILABILITY Spring and summer. Also winter from florists.

CONDITIONING (FRESH) Wrap stems in paper to keep straight and then stand in deep water for several hours.

PICKING FOR DRYING Spring.

DRYING METHODS Dry with desiccant or press petals in flower press.

Typha **Bulrush**

Bulrushes must be picked just as the roll of seeds turns brown, and well before the column starts to break up and deposit its seeds. Treat the surface of the bulrush with hair spray to hold the seeds in position as it dries.

AVAILABILITY Summer.

CONDITIONING (FRESH) Stand in deep water for several hours.

PICKING FOR DRYING Summer.

DRYING METHODS Air dry by standing in container without water.

Verbena

A large range of annual and perennial plants mainly pink, mauve and purple. Some are short-stemmed but others are very tall (*V. bonariensis*). Some varieties are scented. Last very well in water.

AVAILABILITY Summer, autumn.

CONDITIONING (FRESH) Stand in deep water for several hours.

PICKING FOR DRYING Summer and autumn.

DRYING METHODS Press individual flowers in flower press.

Verticordia **Feather flower**

The strong-shaped, large, flat combs of flowers, which dry easily, add an interesting texture to arrangements.

AVAILABILITY Summer.

CONDITIONING (FRESH) Slit and recut stems and then stand in deep water for several hours.

PICKING FOR DRYING Summer.

DRYING METHODS Air dry by hanging.

Viburnum

Evergreen and deciduous shrubs with white or pink flowers, often heavily scented. Not suitable for preserving.

AVAILABILITY Winter, spring and autumn.

CONDITIONING (FRESH) Remove all leaves of *V. opulus* (European cranberry). Scrape, slit and recut stems and then stand in deep water for several hours. Dip stem ends of all viburnums in boiling water when leaves are young or in flower.

Vinca **Periwinkle**

Evergreen trailing plants with blue, mauve or white flowers. *V. difformis* has white or pale-blue flowers in midwinter.

AVAILABILITY Winter, spring and summer.

CONDITIONING (FRESH) Stand in deep water for several hours.

PICKING FOR DRYING Winter to summer.

DRYING METHODS Press flowers in flower press or dry in desiccant.

Viola **Pansy, viola, violet**

Varying sizes of the well-known viola-shaped flowers in a wide range of colors. All are short-stemmed. Some varieties are fragrant, and are delicious to eat, in desserts and cakes, when crystallized.

AVAILABILITY Spring to autumn. Some pansies all year.

CONDITIONING (FRESH) Stand in deep water for several hours.

PICKING FOR DRYING Spring.

DRYING METHODS Press in flower press or crystallize.

Vitis **Grape**

Can be used for the foliage, particularly with autumn color, or for the fruit. Vines can be twisted together in lengths of about 4 feet to form rustic wreaths. Bend into shape before vines dry.

AVAILABILITY Autumn.

CONDITIONING (FRESH) Foliage: dip stem ends in boiling water and then stand in deep water for several hours. Fruit: avoid removing the bloom.

PICKING FOR DRYING Winter.

DRYING METHODS Air dry by standing in container in a little water or press autumnal leaves in flower press.

Xeranthemum **Immortelle**

The papery flowers of immortelle will dry on the plant, but they are delicate and often get damaged if dried in this way.

AVAILABILITY Summer.

CONDITIONING (FRESH) Stand in deep water for several hours.

PICKING FOR DRYING Summer.

DRYING METHODS Air dry by hanging.

Zantedeschia **Arum lily, calla lily**

Pure white, folded trumpets with a central spike. Large glossy leaves. Some people regard them as being funereal. Pink and yellow varieties also available. Not suitable for drying.

AVAILABILITY Spring and early summer.

CONDITIONING (FRESH) Stand in deep water for several hours.

Zea mays **Decorative corn, Indian corn, maize, sweet corn**

Grass with large leaves and large yellow seedheads wrapped in green and topped with soft tassels. The 'Rainbow' variety produces a selection of small, multi-colored seedheads which are not edible.

AVAILABILITY Autumn.

CONDITIONING (FRESH) If height required, push a stick into the base of seedheads quickly because they dry out.

PICKING FOR DRYING Autumn.

DRYING METHODS Air dry by standing in container without water.

Zinnia

Very colourful annuals with large double, daisylike flowerheads available in yellow, orange, red, purple, green or white. Last well in water.

AVAILABILITY Summer, autumn.

CONDITIONING (FRESH) Stand in deep water for several hours.

PICKING FOR DRYING Summer.

DRYING METHODS Dry with desiccant.

INDEX

Figures in italic refer to illustrations.

ACKNOWLEDGMENTS

Designers: Mick Keates, Hilary Krag
Editors: Mary Davies, Catherine Tilley
Illustrators: Will Giles, Sandra Pond
Studio: Del and Co
Typesetter: Bournetype, Bournemouth
Reproduction: Colourscan, Singapore

Dorling Kindersley
Managing editor: Jemima Dunne
Managing art editor: Derek Coombes
Editorial assistance: Candida Ross-Macdonald, Julia Harris-Voss
Design assistance: Mark Regardsoe
Production: Jeanette Graham

Photographic credits
All photography by Andreas Einsiedel and Stephen Hayward, except: p 10 Alex
Starkey/Country Life; pp 206/207 Tania Midgely